The Western Hemisphere Idea:
Its Rise and Decline

The Western Hemisphere Idea:
Its Rise and Decline

ARTHUR P. WHITAKER

Cornell Paperbacks

CORNELL UNIVERSITY PRESS

ITHACA AND LONDON

CORNELL UNIVERSITY PRESS

First published 1954
First printing, Cornell Paperbacks, 1965
Second printing 1969

Standard Book Number 8014-9001-4
Library of Congress Catalog Card Number 54-13291

PRINTED IN THE UNITED STATES OF AMERICA
BY VALLEY OFFSET, INC.

Preface

THE eight essays which follow are in the main identical with the eight Commonwealth Foundation Lectures that I gave at University College, London, in January and February 1953. I have, however, made a good many changes in matters of detail, partly by way of clarification and correction and partly in order to domesticate the foreign lectures and put them in a form more suitable for publication. Among other things, I have added footnote citations and a list of the works cited. These serve the twofold purpose of acknowledging my indebtedness for direct quotations and major facts and ideas and of providing the interested reader with a few signposts to the literature of the subject.

The body of this literature is massive, for these eight essays deal with key developments in the history of an important idea over a long period of time and in a large geographical area. The period extends from the eighteenth century, when the idea took shape, to the mid-twentieth century, by which time it seems to have lost its hold in the United States. The area covered includes not only the United States and Latin America, where the idea has had most of its development, but also Canada, where it has received some attention, and still more Western Europe, which laid the groundwork for it and made a great, if only negative or indirect, contribution to its subsequent growth and ultimate decline.

While the reader is referred to the first essay for a definition of the Western Hemisphere idea, here at the outset he should be urged to keep constantly in mind a distinction which is vital to an understanding of all that follows. This is the distinction between the politico-geographical idea in question and the shifting and imperfect forms in which it has been given political expression, such as the Monroe Doctrine, the Drago Doctrine, the Panama Congress, and Pan Americanism.

This distinction is not only one of the fundamental terms of the present work, it is also one of its chief claims to whatever novelty it may possess. Masterly studies of the Monroe Doctrine and Pan Americanism have already been made by historians of both the Americas, such as Dexter Perkins and Joseph B. Lockey of the United States, John P. Humphrey of Canada, Alejandro M. Alvarez of Chile, Enrique Gil of Argentina, Helio Lobo of Brazil, and Jesús M. Yepes of Colombia; but these belong rather to the history of politics and diplomacy than to the history of ideas. To be sure, these two aspects of history overlap, and it is precisely the area of their overlapping that is examined in the present volume. This is what distinguishes it sharply from the talented Mexican historian Leopoldo Zea's very recent book, *América como conciencia* (1953). The latter is primarily concerned with the quest for an American philosophy and pays relatively little attention to politics, diplomacy, and economics, which bulk large in the following pages.

The reader is also invited to take note of what I have not

tried to do. These essays make no pretense whatever to giving an account either of Latin American policies toward the United States or of the latter's policy toward Latin America. I have drawn heavily on works in this field by Samuel Flagg Bemis, J. Fred Rippy, and many other specialists in North and South America; but I have drawn from them only the materials that fit into the very different design of this book. Finally, I have not undertaken to give a complete history even of the Western Hemisphere idea. Rather, I have focused attention on what seemed to me the key stages of its checkered career and on its most interesting exponents and critics at the various stages, sketching in the intervals and the background only to the extent that seemed indispensable for continuity and perspective.

There is no more pretense to finality in the text of these essays than to exhaustiveness in the citations. To give the work this quality would require a study many times larger than this one. My purpose is much more modest. I regard these essays as nothing more than a pioneer sketch whose merit will consist mainly in whatever stimulus it may give to the discussion of the idea with which the essays deal. Even those who do not subscribe to Señor Zea's proposition that "all crises are crises of ideas" will doubtless agree that the time has come when historians ought to study more closely the development of an idea which has played an important part in the history of the Western World for the past century and a half but is now in a state of crisis.

ARTHUR P. WHITAKER

Philadelphia, Pennsylvania
March 1954

Contents

The Western Hemisphere Idea:
Its Rise and Decline

I

Meaning and Origin of the

Western Hemisphere Idea

FROM its emergence in the late eighteenth and early nineteenth century to the present, the core of the Western Hemisphere idea has been the proposition that the peoples of this Hemisphere stand in a special relationship to one another which sets them apart from the rest of the world. This core binds together expressions of the idea otherwise so diverse as the unilateral Monroe Doctrine of 1823, the economic corollary to that doctrine proposed by Argentine Foreign Minister Drago in 1902, and the evolving Pan American movement since 1889.

Meaning

As these examples suggest, the primary connotation of the idea is political, and, as the term "Western Hemisphere" suggests, an essential ingredient of it is a geographical concept. But at an early date a large cluster of related ideas, social and cultural as well as politico-geographical, and mystical as well as rational, began to grow up about it. Thus, as early as 1813 Thomas Jefferson was writing that the unity of the American peoples extended to all their "modes of existence." [1] During the next decade this belief was fortified by the Latin American struggle for independence, which paralleled that of the United States and produced a group of new states whose political institutions and ideas in many respects resembled and were even modeled upon those of the United States. So it was that in 1826 the Mexican statesman Lucas Alamán declared that while nature had made the countries of America neighbors, "the similarity of their political institutions has bound them even more closely together, strengthening in them the dominion of just and liberal principles." [2]

The contrast, real or supposed, between all of America and all of Europe was one of the basic assumptions of the Western Hemisphere idea, both in Alamán's generation and later. Consequently, the proposition that the American peoples were "set apart from the rest of the world" meant primarily "set apart from Europe." This notion was expressed with varying degrees of intensity. In North America it found comparatively mild expression in Monroe's classic declaration of 1823. In South America, Simón Rodríguez, tutor to the Liberator, Simón Bolívar, voiced it more strongly in his description of Europe as "a bright veil covering the most horrible picture of misery and vice." [3]

With the passage of time, antagonism toward Europe diminished, though it never entirely disappeared. Otherwise, the idea retained all its original characteristics well into the

[1] See below, p. 28.
[2] Arthur P. Whitaker, *The United States and the Independence of Latin America* (Baltimore, 1941), p. 569, n. 17. Cited hereafter as *Independence*.
[3] Leopoldo Zea, *América como conciencia* (Mexico, 1953), p. 130.

twentieth century. In December 1915, while President Wilson labored on his Pan American Pact, Secretary of State Robert Lansing, addressing the Second Pan American Scientific Congress, stated the idea in the familiar triple terms of "geographical isolation," "similar political institutions," and a "common conception of human rights." [4]

On the same occasion an even stronger statement of it was made by a young lawyer, John Foster Dulles, who was to become Secretary of State in 1953. Dulles' statement was so carefully considered and illustrates so well the rational-mystical character of the idea that it deserves to be quoted at length. Discussing the question, "Are there specific American problems of international law?" Dulles said:

Underlying the question which is the subject of discussion, there is a concept which I would consider—namely, that there exists among the American States some sentiment of solidarity, which sets them apart from other nations of the world. . . . Consider on the one hand, the fact that, during the last 90 years, almost a score of . . . international conferences have been held to deal with international problems from the point of view of the American States, and that at no one conference has a non-American nation participated or been invited to participate. Consider, on the other hand, that at none of the international congresses held during the same period at which European nations have participated have the American States generally joined in, except at the Second Hague Peace Conference.

Such a state of facts can not be explained as accidental. It is charged with significance. It points indeed to the existence of some powerful underlying cause. This cause I believe to be what the late Senhor Nabuco [Joaquim Nabuco, Ambassador of Brazil to the United States] so admirably expressed as "the sentiment of our own separate orbit, of an orbit absolutely detached from the European in which Africa and Asia, not speaking of Australasia, are

[4] John Bassett Moore, *The Principles of American Diplomacy* (New York, 1918), p. 400.

3

moving." . . . The vigor of this sentiment is strikingly attested by its persistence for so long a time and throughout so great a territory . . . in spite of a comparative lack of commercial and social intercourse between many of the American States. . . . It must be recognized as a force to be taken account of irrespective of speculation as to the logic of its existence.[5]

The rest of Dulles' address assumed the existence among the American states of this sentiment of "a common personality, distinguishing them from the other nations of the world." Reasoning on this basis, he went so far as to suggest that, in order to exclude non-American nations from the settlement of problems of the Caribbean danger zone, the American states develop a system of what would now be called multilateral intervention and which he described as a "quasi-trustee" arrangement.

In the United States, as we shall see, the Western Hemisphere idea has lost its hold since the 1930's, and now most of its leading exponents are Latin Americans. As recently as 1952 one of these, the distinguished Mexican writer and diplomat Luis Quintanilla, stated the idea in almost its pristine purity.

We, in the Western Hemisphere, belong to a community of neighbors. . . . Not only do geographical closeness and similar historical backgrounds bring us together, but we all share in common an idea about the organization of society and of the world. In other words, to face the fact of America is to glance at any map. From pole to pole, from ocean to ocean, we are all in the same boat, we were created to live together.[6]

Here, expressed or implied, are almost all the familiar ingredients: the appearance of geographical unity which until

[5] Second Pan American Scientific Congress, *Proceedings*, VII (Washington, D.C., 1917), 687–692.
[6] *Pan Americanismo* (Pan American Association of Philadelphia), November 1952, p. 1.

recently has been given to the Americas by maps, the common experiences of adaptation to a New World environment and a struggle for independence from Europe, and common institutions and ideas. The only feature of the classic idea that this statement omits is the antithesis of Europe versus America, which was its most essential feature during the nineteenth century.

The Western Hemisphere idea was, in fact, born of, and nourished by, the determination to insulate America from Western Europe and its perpetual broils. Yet, paradoxically, the roots of this anti-European idea lie deep in America's European past, while forces arising in Britain and on the Continent have powerfully affected its development and expression from its first formulation down to the present day. Consequently, in the following pages the dominant theme of the growth of the Western Hemisphere "complex" is frequently interrupted by the strongly contrasting theme of the interplay between Europe and America, until, at the close, the latter prevails.

This latest phase presents an apparent contradiction between the decline of the Hemisphere idea and the simultaneous strengthening of Pan American instruments and agencies. The contradiction disappears, however, when one recalls that American regionalism has now been linked with a world-wide system, whereas the essence of the Hemisphere idea is that of a special relationship apart from the rest of the world. As this instance suggests, the distinction between the idea and its various political expressions, whether in Pan Americanism, the Monroe Doctrine, the Drago Doctrine, or other ways, should be kept constantly in mind.

Far from claiming that the Western Hemisphere idea ever enjoyed universal acceptance among the American peoples, we shall show that at all times there has been strong dissent from it. Nevertheless, since the beginning of Latin American

independence it has enjoyed sufficiently widespread acceptance to entitle it to consideration as one of the basic assumptions in the conduct of the relations of the American states
with one another and with the rest of the world.

"A new world to European curiosity"

The Western Hemisphere idea was first formulated by
Americans and in the political terms of an exclusively American system early in the nineteenth century, but it grew out
of the far older conception of America as a New World.
Wholly European in its origin, this conception remained almost exclusively European in its development down to the
eighteenth century.

The truth of this proposition should be obvious the moment
one breaks "New World" down into its two component parts.
One of these was of course the newness of America; the other
was the congruity of the various parts of America. The idea
of the newness of America was obviously an importation from
Europe; the "wild surmise" with which European explorers
first viewed America and its adjacent waters was not shared
by any of its native peoples. To the latter, the New World
was Europe. More than two centuries after Balboa, Dr. Samuel Johnson put the case in a nutshell when he said that
Columbus "gave a new world to European curiosity." [7] Although in Dr. Johnson's time the ethnic composition of the
peoples of America had been greatly altered by more than
two centuries of immigration and amalgamation, it was still
as true in the mid-eighteenth century as at the beginning of
the sixteenth century that any American of whatever origin
who regarded America as a New World was looking at it
through European eyes.

Likewise, the idea of the congruity of the various parts of

[7] Quoted in Pedro Henríquez-Ureña, *Literary Currents in Hispanic America* (Cambridge, 1945), p. 4.

6

America—the idea that America possessed a unity of any kind —was one which, before the arrival of the Europeans, had never occurred to anyone in all the agglomeration of atomistic societies that inhabited America from Alaska to the Tierra del Fuego. This, too, was an idea which came from looking at America through a European perspective as it was represented on European maps, which was brought to America by Europeans, and which was held only by that part of the American people whose culture was of European origin. To this day it has not been adopted by the remnants of the indigenous cultures that still survive on a considerable scale in various parts of America; to them, Pan Americanism is gibberish.

Moreover, even among Americans of European origin this half of the Western Hemisphere idea, congruity, proved far more difficult to acclimatize than the other half, the New World idea.[8] The latter, transplanted to America by the first discoverers and colonizers, flourished there from the start, for the essentially European sense of the freshness, the newness, of the New World was constantly renewed by the continuing process of exploration and colonization, which was not completed in any large part of America until the nineteenth century and is still incomplete in some parts of it. But this same process produced the opposite effect in the case of the equally European idea of all-American unity or congruity, for its effect upon the new communities of European origin, as formerly upon the pre-Columbian peoples, was to diversify and atomize: witness the fact that the former American dominion of a single European power, Spain, is now divided into eighteen separate, sovereign, highly diversified, and frequently jarring nations.

[8] For a fuller discussion of this subject, see my essay, "The Americas in the Atlantic Triangle," in *Ensayos sobre la historia del Nuevo Mundo* (Mexico City, 1951), pp. 69–96.

7

Added to the atomizing influence of the environment was the diversity brought to the New World from across the Atlantic, for America was the offspring of a Europe divided by the Protestant-Catholic schism and by the wars of religion that ensued for more than a hundred years. This was precisely the period when the foundations of western culture were brought to North and South America; and the two chief founding powers in America, England and Spain, represented the opposite extremes in the Old World mêlée. The conquest of Mexico was begun two years after Martin Luther posted his ninety-five theses on the church door at Wittenberg; Peru was conquered while Henry VIII was having himself made supreme head of the Church of England; the unsuccessful first English settlement in America was made just before Philip II sent his Spanish Armada against England; and the beginnings of successful English settlement in America were made in Virginia a decade before, and in Massachusetts in the first decade after, the beginning of the Thirty Years' War.

Commercial and political rivalry among the European colonizing powers made the rifts in the New World deep and lasting. No part of America lived isolated from the rest of the world; but in all parts of it the orientation of culture and sentiment as well as of trade and politics, of interest as well as of interests, was across the Atlantic toward Europe. Reflecting the divisions of Europe, the various parts of America had no unity among themselves. According to John Quincy Adams, a close student of his country's foreign relations, the United States still had at the close of the eighteenth century "no more intercourse" with most of the rest of America "than with the inhabitants of another planet." [9]

Adams exaggerated the novelty of the discovery of each

[9] Message to the House of Representatives, March 15, 1826, in James D. Richardson, ed., *Letters and Papers of the Presidents,* II (Washington, D.C., 1896), 337–338.

other by the two Americas, but this was in fact of such recent occurrence that the novelty had not completely worn off when he spoke of it in 1826. Thomas Jefferson, whose interest in Latin America antedated Adams', could still declare in 1810, apropos of Alexander von Humboldt's just published *Political Essay on New Spain* (Mexico), that that country, so near the United States, had been "almost locked up from the knowledge of man hitherto." [10] And conversely, until shortly before Jefferson wrote this, the Latin Americans' ignorance about the United States had been abysmal.

The process by which the Americas discovered one another and developed the New World idea into the Western Hemisphere idea was not completed until the early years of the nineteenth century. It was slow because it was complicated. It involved not only the acquisition of knowledge, but also the development of a new feeling, the feeling of Americanism in the continental, hemispheric sense. Knowledge alone was not enough. The reading public in America as well as in Europe was learning a great deal in this period about many parts of the world from writers as varied as the Abbé Raynal, Captain Cook and Humboldt. But no more in America than in Europe did the reader necessarily identify himself and his community with the new lands and peoples thus brought within his ken. That happened only when Americans were learning about America.

The process in question took place in two stages, which we may designate as first the provincial and then the continental stage, or, in terms that apply to a later date, first the national and then the inter-American stage.

In the first, or provincial, stage, the colonist or creole began to think of himself as belonging to his part of America; he was no longer simply a European-in-America. The feeling did not necessarily have political implications of revolution

[10] Quoted in Whitaker, *Independence,* p. 27.

9

and national independence. Indeed, in some cases, instead of leading to an effort at independence, the feeling grew out of the effort. Such was the case of Benjamin Franklin, who always thought of himself as an Englishman until, after he had reached the age of sixty, he found that the logic of his defense of his rights as an Englishman forced him to become an American.

Interestingly enough, in Latin America, where the independence movement developed much later than in the United States, we learn from the historians of that area that at least some of its people developed this sense of Americanism much earlier. Thus, a prominent Brazilian historian dates its first rise in his country from the resistance of its people to the Dutch intrusion in the second quarter of the seventeenth century; [11] some evidence of its existence in sixteenth-century New Granada (Colombia) has just been published; [12] and in Peru clear expressions of it are to be found in the works of the historian-geographer Eusebio Llano Zapata about 1750 and also in the well-known travel book written about 1770 by the mestizo Concolorcorvo.[13] In all these cases, however, the sense of Americanism was purely provincial, if not parochial; there was nothing continental about it. Even in Britain's North American colonies as late as 1765, a new note was struck when one of the delegates to the Stamp Act Congress, Christopher Gadsden, exhorted his colleagues: "There ought to be no New England man, no New Yorker, known on the continent, but all of us Americans." [14] And of course by

[11] Pedro Calmon, *Historia de la civilización brasileña* (Buenos Aires, 1938), pp. 77–78.

[12] Juan Friede, "El arraigo histórico del espíritu de independencia en el Nuevo Reino de Granada," *Revista de Historia de América,* no. 33 (1952), pp. 95–104.

[13] Concolorcorvo, *El lazarillo de ciegos caminantes* (Biblioteca de Cultura Peruana, Primera Série, no. 6, Paris, 1938), "Nota Preliminar," p. 8.

[14] Quoted in S. E. Morison and H. S. Commager, *The Growth of the American Republic* (New York, 1937), p. 29.

America Gadsden meant, not the whole New World, but only that part of British America which later became the United States.

The Enlightenment

In its first, or provincial, stage, therefore, the rise of Americanism tended toward a further fragmentation of America through the development of many local loyalties which signified a weakening of ties with Europe but did not bind the fragments together in a new synthesis. This synthesis was achieved in a second and quite different stage and under a stimulus, provided mainly by Europe, which took the form of three eighteenth-century revolutions: the intellectual, the commercial, and the political.

The intellectual revolution was accomplished by the spread of the Enlightenment. Historians of the Age of the Enlightenment, such as Carl Becker and Ernst Cassirer,[15] have quite properly focused their attention upon its development in Western Europe; but in any history of it which takes account of its significance in world history, much attention must also be devoted to the spread of the Enlightenment to North and South America. To the historian of the Americas, the importance of its extension to his part of the world is of course still greater; and for the particular aspect of American history with which we are concerned, namely, the emergence of the Western Hemisphere idea, its influence was decisive.

The Enlightenment spread to all the countries across the Atlantic, first to the United States and somewhat later to Latin America;[16] and in both it fell on fertile soil. Americans,

[15] Carl Becker, *The Heavenly City of the Eighteenth-Century Philosophers* (New Haven, 1932); Ernst Cassirer, *The Philosophy of the Enlightenment* (Princeton, 1951).

[16] Arthur P. Whitaker, ed., *Latin America and the Enlightenment* (New York, 1942). Cited hereafter as *Enlightenment*.

11

both North and South, were attracted somewhat by the "completely original form of philosophic thought" which it produced, but still more by its gospel of reform and progress through the promotion of useful knowledge.

Among the most important agencies in spreading the Enlightenment, in America as in Europe, were the academies or learned societies which sprang up in the course of the eighteenth century. The first such body in the New World, and one of the most important, was organized at Philadelphia in 1746. Benjamin Franklin was one of its founders, and it bore a name that left no room for doubt about its being an offspring of the Enlightenment, for it was called "The American Philosophical Society for Promoting Useful Knowledge" —the name it still goes by today. The corresponding bodies in Spanish America, which began to be organized about 1790 and enjoyed the royal government's good will if not its support, were usually given names similar to those of their prototypes that had appeared in many parts of Spain since about 1760, such as "Patriotic Society," or "Society of Friends of Their Country," with perhaps the prefix "Economic," as in the case of the first of them, the "Sociedad Económica de Amigos del País" of Havana, which, like its Philadelphia counterpart, is still very much alive today.

Where the promotion of useful knowledge was concerned, the Spanish government, particularly under the "enlightened despot" Charles III (1759–1788), and to a lesser extent the government of Portugal too, not only permitted but subsidized the transfer of the Enlightenment to Latin America. Sometimes this took the form of aid to scientists, either to those already in Latin America or to others who were sent there by the home government. An example of the latter kind of aid was provided by the related missions of Spanish and German metallurgists and mineralogists sent to Mexico, Colombia, and Peru in 1788 by the Spanish government.[17] So eager was the latter for the success of these scientific missions that in order to attract personnel of the best possible quality it not only engaged foreigners but also guaranteed the Protestants among them religious toleration in Spanish America. By these and other means, Madrid did achieve a large measure of success in promoting useful knowledge in its American dominions. For example, by 1800 José Celestino Mutis of Bogotá had won world-wide renown by his botanical studies; and Alexander von Humboldt, after a five years' residence in Spanish America and the United States (1799–1804), concluded that there was no better center for scientific studies in America than the one in Mexico City.

Understandably, evidence regarding the propagation of the more controversial aspects of the Enlightenment in Latin America, such as those associated with the names of Voltaire and Rousseau, is not easy to obtain, but enough is available to destroy the long-accepted myth that colonial Latin America was sealed off from the rest of the world by a Chinese Wall, or in modern parlance, an iron curtain. In fact, according to a leading authority on this question, J. T. Lanning, by 1800 Spanish America was abreast of the most advanced thought of the Enlightenment in Europe.[18] Perhaps the best supporting evidence is provided by the fact that, as soon as the independence movement in Spanish America began, its leaders revealed a familiarity with the works of the eighteenth-century philosophers which betokened long acquaintance with them. Moreover, most of the leading American expo-

---

[17] For a recent account of the important mission to Mexico, with references, see Clement G. Motten, *Mexican Silver and the Enlightenment* (Philadelphia, 1950), and for the origin of the three missions, Arthur P. Whitaker, "The Elhuyar Mining Missions and the Enlightenment," *Hispanic American Historical Review*, XXXI (1951), 557–585.
[18] See Whitaker, *Enlightenment,* pp. 89–90.

nents of the Enlightenment took the patriot side in the struggle for independence. In short, the Enlightenment was a stimulus to Americanism. This was one of its major contributions to the growth of the Western Hemisphere idea.

It was not the only such stimulus, in Latin America any more than in the United States. For example, insofar as Spanish America is concerned, there is much to be said for the thesis recently developed by certain Hispanic historians, such as Camilo Barcia Trelles and Manuel Giménez Fernández of Spain and Silvio Zavala of Mexico,[19] that a strong stimulus was provided by the liberal Catholic tradition transmitted through Spain itself. But in evaluating this thesis for our purpose, two points should be kept in mind. First, after declining in the seventeenth century, the liberal Catholic-Spanish tradition was revived during the period of the Enlightenment and was most effective when fused with it—as it was, for instance, in Viscardo y Guzmán's famous *Letter to the Spanish Americans,* which was published in London in 1801 and is the chief exhibit in the case as stated by Giménez Fernández. Second, this fusion contributed to the growth of the Western Hemisphere idea by making it easier for the peoples of Anglo-America and Spanish America to believe that they shared a common political philosophy.

In the foregoing brief survey, stress has been laid upon Latin America's share in the Enlightenment rather than that of the United States because there seems to be no need to argue the case of the country that produced Benjamin Franklin and Thomas Jefferson.

The Enlightenment not only created for the first time a basic kinship of ideas between the two Americas, it also gave

[19] Camilo Barcia Trelles, "Doctrina de Monroe y cooperación internacional," in Académie de Droit International, *Recueil des cours, 1930,* II (Paris, 1931), 391–605; Manuel Giménez Fernández, *Las doctrinas populistas en la independencia de Hispano-América* (Seville, 1947); Silvio Zavala, *La filosofía política en la conquista de América* (Mexico City, 1947).

them for the first time a reciprocal interest in, and some knowledge about, each other's culture. At the beginning of the eighteenth century, the attitude of both sides was typified by Cotton Mather, whose only interest in Spanish America was a missionary one—to convert the papists to Protestantism. The new attitude which both sides were beginning to take as the century came to a close was illustrated by the fact that even in the wilds of Venezuela Alexander von Humboldt encountered a Spanish American scientist who was familiar with the works of Benjamin Franklin. By 1800 the American Philosophical Society had established relations with scientists in Mexico and Cuba, and in 1801 and 1802 the *Gazeta de Guatemala* took extensive notice of medical studies recently published by Drs. Benjamin Rush and Benjamin Smith Barton of Philadelphia. In 1808 the Peruvian José Hipólito Unánue published a book on the climate of Lima (*El clima de Lima*) which contains several references to the New York periodical *Medical Repository*.[20]

Admittedly, instances of this kind were not numerous even at the turn of the century, but the rapidity with which they multiplied after the Spanish Americans began to achieve independence is proof that the ground had been well prepared. Thus, efforts to promote inter-American cultural relations were made in 1817 by the New York Lyceum of Natural History and in the 1820's by Jared Sparks, editor of the *North American Review;* both were warmly reciprocated in Latin America, and among Sparks's correspondents were cultural leaders of the stature of the Mexican Lucas Alamán, the Colombian José Manuel Restrepo, and the Argentine Manuel Moreno.

The spread of this vital new force thus prepared the way for the crystallization of the Western Hemisphere idea by

[20] The information in this paragraph was drawn mainly from Harry Bernstein, *Origins of Inter-American Interest, 1700–1812* (Philadelphia, 1945).

15

providing both the Americas for the first time in history with the cultural basis for a common understanding and with the means to develop it. But as a parallel development occurred in Europe, bridging the gap opened in the sixteenth century between Protestant and Catholic countries, the first effect of the spread of the Enlightenment was to strengthen the ties between Europe and America,[21] for it created a feeling of fellowship among enlightened people in all the countries comprised in the so-called Atlantic Triangle—the sides of which were formed by Western Europe, the United States, and Latin America. This was the kind of thing the hopeful philosophers of that age looked forward to when they spoke of the international "Republic of Letters" and called themselves "citizens of the world." Not until the Atlantic Triangle was split in two in the early nineteenth century were international-minded Americans fully converted to the view that they were citizens of only half a world.

The anti-American thesis

There was, however, one other development arising out of the Enlightenment that aided in bringing about the new hemispheric orientation. This was the elaboration by European writers in the second half of the eighteenth century of what we may call an anti-American thesis and the defensive reaction which this thesis not unnaturally provoked among the victims of their denigration.[22]

The anti-American thesis may be summed up in the propo-

---

[21] Michael Kraus, *The Atlantic Civilization: Eighteenth-Century Origins* (Ithaca, 1949). On the European intellectual background see Paul Hazard, *La pensée européene du XVIIIème siècle* (Paris, 1946), and on the aspect indicated Gilbert Chinard, "Eighteenth Century Theories on America as a Human Habitat," American Philosophical Society, *Proceedings,* XCI, no. 1 (1947), 27–57.

[22] Antonello Gerbi, *Viejas polémicas sobre el nuevo mundo* (3d ed., Lima, 1946), and Zea, *América como conciencia,* ch. vii, "Nacimiento de una conciencia americana."

sition that the New World was inferior to the old in every respect as to both man and nature. Its development betokened a new attitude toward America on the part of Europe and was clearly a product of the new spirit of the Enlightenment. In the sixteenth and seventeenth centuries European writers had made no such generalized comparison, either favorable or unfavorable, of America with Europe. To them, the newness of the New World did not give it either uniqueness or unity; rather, as Henríquez-Ureña has pointed out, they considered it in terms of a problem which was universal and which the European mind of the Renaissance was already debating when America was discovered, namely, "the age-old contrast between nature and culture." [23] The results of the inquiry were mixed, for if it produced the cult of the noble savage, it also produced the cult of the ignoble savage; in both cases the American savage was judged not as an American but as a savage.

Nor was any such generalized comparison implicit in the tendency of Europeans of that earlier period to think of America in utopian terms. Sir Thomas More and Tommaso Campanella chose America as the locus of their utopias, and about 1540 the Spanish-born Bishop Vasco de Quiroga actually established two utopian communities in Mexico.[24] It would be a great mistake, however, to regard these utopias as turning the eighteenth-century judgment upside down and exalting America above Europe. The utopians merely believed that America provided a more favorable environment for the application of ideas that were thoroughly European. When they thought about the native peoples of America at all, they were sure that these stood quite as sorely in need of reform as did the peoples of Europe. This con-

[23] Henríquez-Ureña, *op. cit.*, p. 14.
[24] Silvio Zavala, *La Utopia de Tomás More en la Nueva España y otros estudios* (Mexico City, 1937).

viction was strongly stressed by Vasco de Quiroga, the only one of the three writers who either saw America with his own eyes or actually tried to put Utopia into practice. In short, the sixteenth and seventeenth centuries did not produce the antithesis "Europe versus America."

Eighteenth-century Europe did produce it, in the form of that denigration of America to which reference has already been made. This resulted from the combination of a typical intellectual effort of the Enlightenment with an eighteenth-century European's perhaps unavoidable misinformation about America. The effort in question was that of the French naturalist Buffon to achieve a scientific classification of nature, particularly by distinguishing between different species of animals. Undeterred by his very imperfect knowledge of America, he included it in his study and set forth his conclusions about it dogmatically and in detail. His general thesis was that "animated nature is much less active, much less varied, and much less strong" in America, so that not only were plants and animals smaller in America, but those taken to it from Europe degenerated there.

Many anticipations of Buffon in certain details can be found in earlier writers, but he was the first to present the thesis in a comprehensive, systematic, and apparently scientific way. Because of its novelty and his prestige it made a great impression on both sides of the Atlantic. In Europe it was echoed in several widely read books of the next generation. It received its most notable expression in Cornelius de Pauw's *Recherches philosophiques sur les Américains* (1768) in which the author maintained that everything in America was "either degenerate or monstrous," its men cowardly and impotent, its iron of such poor quality that not even nails could be made of it, and its dogs unable to bark. In somewhat less extreme form, this notion was given its widest publicity by Abbé Raynal's *Histoire philosophique,* which between its

18

publication in 1770 and 1800 passed through more than fifty editions and became, in Horace Walpole's phrase, "the Bible of two worlds."

The Americanist reaction

So far as this Hemisphere was concerned, Raynal's book was certainly not the Bible of the New World. Indignant replies to the anti-American thesis came from many an American pen, including those of Father Molina, in his *History of Chile* (1776); Father Clavigero, in his *History of Mexico* (1780); Thomas Jefferson, in his *Notes on Virginia* (1785); Philip Freneau and Joel Barlow, in their poem *Anarchiad* (1786); and Alexander Hamilton, in *The Federalist* papers (1788). These few illustrations are enough to give some idea of how widespread the reaction was in America, and it should be noted that these works are the first in which American writers, North or South, had ever made a general comparison of America with Europe. It was from European writers that Americans learned to think in terms of an antithesis between America and Europe.

This Americanist trend was strengthened by the commercial revolution, and still more by the political revolution, which began to sweep over the whole Atlantic world in the eighteenth century.[25] Of these we shall have to speak much more briefly than we did of the intellectual revolution, since they concern us only insofar as they helped to shape the growth of the Western Hemisphere idea.

The aspect of the commercial revolution that concerns us is the development of a large-scale and almost entirely new nexus of trade relations between the United States and the whole of Latin America. In 1700 the English colonies which were later to become the United States had virtually no trade

[25] For the European side of it between 1763 and 1789, see Leo Gershoy, *From Despotism to Revolution, 1763–1789* (New York, 1944), pp. 39–47.

relations with even the nearest Spanish colonies, such as Cuba and Mexico. By 1800 merchant ships flying the Stars and Stripes were frequenting all the principal ports of Spanish America and Brazil and carrying on all kinds of commerce there, including such specialized branches as whaling and the slave trade. This commerce provided the means of political and cultural intercourse between the Americas. It was contraband in time of peace, but both Spain and Portugal legalized it in time of war. Spain was at war many times in the eighteenth century, including the greater part of the two decades which began with its declaration of war on the regicide French Republic in 1793 and ended with the expulsion of the "intruder King" Joseph Bonaparte and the restoration of Ferdinand VII, an absolute monarch and one of those Bourbons who had learned nothing and forgotten nothing in a whole generation of world war and revolution.

The revolutionary age, which was a common experience of the whole Atlantic world between 1775 and 1850, had its profoundest effects on the American portion in the first half-century, ending in 1825. By this time the United States and the area covered by nineteen of the present twenty Latin American states had won their independence. The crucial decade for our purpose was the one which began in 1808 with the French intrusion into Spain, where Joseph Bonaparte occupied a throne supported by the bayonets of his brother Napoleon's soldiers.

The events of this decade were the catalytic agent which precipitated the formulation of the Western Hemisphere idea. In the vast area stretching from California to Cape Horn, Spanish American patriots started a struggle for independence which quickened the sense of hemispheric solidarity by its apparent analogy to the recent struggle of the United States against another European power, Great Britain.[26] The Spanish American struggle was hardly well begun when there emerged in Europe that Concert of the great powers, commonly though mistakenly called the Holy Alliance, whose leaders soon took a stand hostile to the very principles on which the independence of every American nation was based and to their whole political way of life—to the right of revolution, popular sovereignty, constitutional and representative government, and personal liberty. That Britain, one of the members of the European Concert, did not underwrite this program, was not clear to Americans until after the catalytic agent had already done its work.

That typical child of the Enlightenment, Benjamin Franklin, had prayed that "a thorough knowledge of the Rights of Man may pervade all nations of the earth, so that a philosopher may set his foot anywhere on its surface and say 'This is my country.'" Early in the nineteenth century many Americans came to feel that the Western Hemisphere was the only part of the world which could answer Franklin's prayer. When they did so, the formation of the Western Hemisphere idea was complete.

[26] It also quickened that sense of the newness of the New World, mentioned at the beginning of this chapter, and discussed in relation to the growth of Manifest Destiny in Albert K. Weinberg, *Manifest Destiny: A Study of Nationalist Expansion in American History* (Baltimore, 1935), pp. 134–135. Cited hereafter as *Manifest Destiny*.

II

Political Expression of the

Idea: The American System

IN THE first quarter of the nineteenth century, the Western Hemisphere idea first achieved political expression through the development of what was then called the American system. Though definitions of the latter term differed on details, they were in agreement on the major point, which was that somehow or other the peoples of the Western Hemisphere were tied together by a special relationship which set them apart from the rest of the world. For obvious reasons this development could not occur until the independence movement, already achieved in the United States, had spread to Latin America—that is, until a large enough part of America had started on the road to nationhood to provide a basis for an American system approximating hemispheric proportions. Once that condition had begun to be fulfilled, as it was after Napoleon's invasion of the Iberian peninsula in 1808, the process of translating the Western Hemisphere idea into political terms moved forward with a rapidity which would hardly have been possible had not the ground already been well prepared.

This essay will describe the principal contributions of Latin America and the United States to this process from its beginning in 1808 to its culmination in the Panama Congress of 1826—the first inter-American conference ever held. Paradoxically, Europe too made an important contribution to the process in a number of ways: by creating a favorable climate of opinion through that eighteenth-century sharpening of the New World–Old World antithesis discussed in the preceding chapter; by presenting for a decade after 1815 that threat to America, loosely referred to as the Holy Alliance, which did more than anything else to create a community of interest and sentiment among the peoples of the New World; by setting the latter an example of international co-operation in the Concert of Europe; and even by helping occasionally—as in the writings of the French publicist Abbé de Pradt—to popularize the idea of the American system in America. Nevertheless, the major contributions to the process in question came largely from America itself, and these are our main concern.

It was a complicated process, involving the interplay of ideas among publicists and statesmen in many highly diversified countries, amid constantly changing conditions in a period of world crisis. Consequently, lest the reader lose himself in its intricacies, he would do well to note that this essay will develop three major propositions. These are: (1) that Latin America took the lead in developing international co-operation in the New World, but not in giving this the hemispheric character of a true American system, (2) that the

23

United States took the lead in developing the idea of such a system, but lagged behind Latin America in implementing it through international action, and (3) that when the American system finally became a basis of United States foreign policy, as it did in the Monroe Doctrine of 1823, it was given a character which it retained for more than a century to come, namely, that of a hemispheric projection of the national policy of isolation laid down in Washington's Farewell Address of 1796.

Latin America: Internationalism

From 1810 on, the internationalist movement was promoted in various ways by statesmen and writers of several Spanish American countries. The promoter most frequently cited is Simón Bolívar of Gran Colombia, or Greater Colombia, which included present-day Colombia, Venezuela, and Ecuador. Indeed, he is often given more of the credit than he deserves. For example, as Argentine historians have pointed out, Mariano Moreno of Buenos Aires anticipated in 1810 the essential points contained in Bolívar's famous Jamaica Letter of 1815, and Bernardo Monteagudo, another product of the Plata region, aided greatly in formulating plans for Bolívar's Panama Congress. Nevertheless, since sustained leadership in the movement during the period under consideration came from Gran Colombia, which was dominated by Bolívar, we may take his thought on the subject as representative.[1]

[1] The leading work on Bolívar's political ideas is still Víctor Andrés Belaúnde's more than twenty-year-old stand-by, *Bolívar and the Political Thought of the Spanish American Revolution* (Baltimore, 1930). Gerhard Masur's recent biography, *Simón Bolívar* (Albuquerque, 1948), makes important contributions on other aspects of Bolívar's life, but is less satisfactory for the problems discussed in the present chapter. Notable among recent works stressing Latin American influence more strongly than I have done are Guillermo Hernández de Alba, "Origen de la doctrina panamericana de la confederación," *Revista de Historia de América*, no. 22 (1946), pp. 367–398, and Francisco Cuevas Cancino, *Bolívar: El ideal panamericano del Libertador* (Mexico City, 1951).

For our purposes, the important point is that Bolívar's plans for international co-operation did not accord with the Western Hemisphere idea. Before the Monroe Doctrine was proclaimed in 1823, his plan embraced only Spanish America in the New World; on the other hand, it extended beyond the Western Hemisphere to provide for some sort of link between Spanish America and Great Britain. On the basis of his Jamaica Letter,[2] he has frequently been credited with holding hemispheric views, for in it he spoke of the possibility that the Isthmus of Panama might become for "America" what ancient Corinth had been for the Grecian states, serving as the seat of a "congress of representatives of republics, kingdoms, and empires that will discuss peace and war with the nations of the world." But the context makes it clear that by "America" he meant only Spanish America,[3] and what is more, the text itself shows that in 1815 he regarded even this narrower notion as a pipe dream.

When Bolívar wrote the Jamaica Letter, he was a beaten rebel and a refugee, but by 1822 the tide had turned in his favor and the dream of 1815 no longer seemed chimerical. Accordingly, he and his Colombian associates, Vice President Santander and Foreign Minister Gual, negotiated a series of bilateral pacts with other Spanish American states which provided for both an immediate alliance and the eventual holding of an international congress.[4] Still, however, as in 1815, his plan embraced only Spanish America in the New World. Moreover, the widening rift between Britain and her other associates in the Concert of Europe now hardened Bolívar's

[2] For the text, see Vicente Lecuna, ed., *Cartas del Libertador* (Caracas, 1929), I, 181–205.

[3] In an understatement, Lockey pointed out many years ago that "the context appears to show that Bolivar here meant Spanish America" (Joseph B. Lockey, *Pan Americanism: Its Beginnings* [New York, 1920], p. 100, n. 41).

[4] Harold A. Bierck, Jr., *Vida pública de don Pedro Gual* (Caracas, 1947), pp. 323–361.

predilection for Britain into a policy. Henceforth it was an essential part of his planning for a Spanish American league that the latter should enjoy the protection of Britain. Given the realities of the power situation in the Atlantic world, this plan may have been the soundest one conceivable, but it had nothing to do with the Western Hemisphere idea and its political expression, the American system.

What effect the Monroe Doctrine had on Bolívar it is impossible to say with certainty. His voluminous published correspondence contains only one rather noncommittal reference to it.[5] Perhaps it is a mere coincidence that shortly after learning about it, he once more began to give his personal attention to the plan for an international conference, which for three years past he had left to Santander and Gual to develop. These two, at any rate, were strongly influenced by Monroe's message, for it certainly stimulated them (as it perhaps did Bolívar) to renewed activity in favor of the proposed international conference, which it was finally agreed should be held at Panama in 1826. The message also brought their planning for the conference more nearly into line with the hemispheric idea of the American system by leading them, first, to invite the United States to participate in the Panama Congress (contrary to Bolívar's original intention) and, second, to supplement the original agenda with a proposal to provide multilateral, inter-American support for the idea of Hemisphere defense which the Monroe Doctrine had stated in unilateral terms.

Bolívar himself, however, was not converted to the American system. An intimate tie with Britain continued to be his chief prescription for Spanish America.[6] In March 1825, as preparations for the Panama Congress were taking shape, he

[5] Lecuna, *op. cit.*, IV, 143, letter dated April 28, 1824.
[6] Germán Cavelier, *La política internacional de Colombia . . . (1820–1830)* (Bogotá, 1949), pp. 70–73.

wrote Santander: "Believe me, my dear General, we shall save the New World if we come to an agreement with England in *political and military matters*. This simple sentence ought to tell you more than two whole volumes." [7]

Despite Bolívar's record, certain historians have claimed for Colombia the credit of pioneering not only the internationalist movement in America but also the idea of a hemispheric American system. Their trump card is the mission of the Colombian envoy to Washington, Manuel Torres, who from early 1821 until shortly before his death in August 1822 is supposed to have given President Monroe and Secretary of State Adams ideas on the latter subject which came to fruition in the Monroe Doctrine of December 1823.[8] The argument is quite unconvincing, if only because there is no reason to believe that a foreign envoy (and an unrecognized one, at that) could have played any important part in persuading Adams and Monroe to adopt an idea which had been anticipated by many persons in the United States, including statesmen of the first rank, during the past decade. Even if it were proved that Torres so persuaded them, the fact would still remain that Torres was not in any real sense a Latin American. Born in Spain, he had been living in Philadelphia for the past quarter-century.

The United States: The Hemisphere idea

The history of the idea of the American system in the United States goes back to the beginning of the republic, and if "America" is understood only in the narrowly national sense, the idea was clearly stated in Washington's Farewell Address of 1796. But our concern is with America in the broader, hemispheric sense, and in this sense the history

[7] Lecuna, *op. cit.*, IV, 288, letter dated March 11, 1825.
[8] Nicolás García Samudio, *Independencia de Hispanoamérica* (Mexico City, 1945), pp. 171–183.

of the idea begins with a letter written in October 1808 by no less a person than President Thomas Jefferson. Replying through a subordinate to overtures from Mexican and Cuban leaders of the incipient independence movement, he wrote: "We consider their interests and ours as the same, and that the object of both must be to exclude all European influence from this hemisphere." [9] To be sure, Jefferson's policy statement makes only a negative application of the Western Hemisphere idea—"the exclusion of all European influence from this hemisphere," but at this same time a positive application of it was made by the ranking general of the United States Army, James Wilkinson, in a letter addressed to Jefferson himself. Wilkinson, who was fond of superlatives, declared that "the grandest spectacle in nature" would be the "liberation of the American continent" from European shackles and the formation of a "distinct community" of American nations.

Jefferson had neither time nor opportunity to develop the implications of the Hemisphere idea before his presidency came to a close a few months later (in March 1809), but in his private correspondence of the next few years he gave it even clearer and more forcible expression. In a letter of 1811 he wrote:

What, in short, is the whole system of Europe towards America but an atrocious and insulting tyranny? One hemisphere of the earth, separated from the other by wide seas on both sides, having a different system of interests flowing from different climates, different soils, different productions, different modes of existence, and its own local relations and duties, is made subservient to all the petty interests of the other, to their laws, their regulations, their passions and wars. [10]

[9] Quoted in Whitaker, *Independence*, p. 43.

[10] Quoted, together with the letter of 1813 (see below in text), in Laura Bornholdt's excellent article, "The Abbé de Pradt and the Monroe Doctrine," *Hispanic American Historical Review*, XXIV (1944), 201–221. The

Two years later he developed the idea still further in a letter to the distinguished savant and expert on Spanish America, Alexander von Humboldt. His text was the independence movement recently begun in New Spain. Though sure that this movement would succeed, Jefferson was not sanguine about the kind of governments it would produce, observing:

History . . . furnishes no example of a priest-ridden people maintaining a free civil government. . . . But in whatever governments they end, they will be *American* governments, no longer to be involved in the never-ceasing broils of Europe. The European nations constitute a separate division of the globe; their localities make them part of a distinct system; they have a set of interests of their own in which it is our business never to engage ourselves. America has a hemisphere to itself. It must have a separate system of interest which must not be subordinated to those of Europe. The insulated state in which nature has placed the American continent should so far avail it that no spark of war kindled in the other quarters of the globe should be wafted across the wide oceans which separate us from them.[11]

These letters of Jefferson's are of the greatest importance for our purpose, for they mark the first full flowering of the Western Hemisphere idea in the American system. The terms in which they describe it are substantially the same as those in which, partly through Jefferson's agency, the American system was incorporated in the Monroe Doctrine ten years later. On that occasion, as we shall see, Monroe used it to give a new turn to the foreign policy of the United States; but he added nothing new to the idea itself. That had already been brought to maturity in Jefferson's letters. They recapitulated the earlier stages of its development, and the letter

text of the Monroe Doctrine and many other documents referred to in the present work will be found in James W. Gantenbein, *The Evolution of Our Latin American Policy: A Documentary Record* (New York, 1950).

[11] See note 10.

to Humboldt carried the idea through another and the final stage by adding a new element, which we may call the mystique of Pan Americanism.

The rational basis of the American system had already been laid when this letter was written. It consisted in the proposition that because of certain definable geographical, political, and other factors, Europe and America constituted separate, distinct, and mutually antagonistic spheres, and each of these spheres possessed an inner unity denoted by the word "system." But, as Jefferson's Humboldt letter shows, he now realized that so far as the American system was concerned, the basis provided by reason was not enough. He had read his friend Humboldt's recent books on Spanish America, and he knew that the same kind of diversities of soil, climate, productions, modes of existence, and behavior that had set America against Europe abounded likewise within America. Obviously, one must admit that they would have the same disrupting influence within the New World itself unless one added a new element transcending reason.

This Jefferson now supplied: it was the magic of the American name. He personified what had hitherto been only a geographical area, for he wrote not "America *is* a separate hemisphere," but "America *has* a separate hemisphere." He then endowed this personified continent with supernatural powers. Though admitting that the odds were against the establishment of free civil governments by the "priest-ridden people" of Spanish America, he was nevertheless satisfied that he had set everything to rights by pointing out that "in whatever governments they end, they will be *American* governments." When we consider that the antithesis of liberty versus despotism was at that time an essential element in the idea of America versus Europe, it is arresting to learn that in Jefferson's view the same antithesis had no bearing upon the relations of the American peoples with one another.

30

All-American unity had now become not a goal but a premise, and it not only existed in defiance of natural laws that operated in other parts of the world, but it also set up different standards of conduct for the peoples within its charmed circle. The mystical idea thus launched by Jefferson in 1813 was to remain one of the chief sources of strength of Pan Americanism throughout the lifetime of the Western Hemisphere idea.

Under Jefferson's successor, James Madison (1809–1817), attention was diverted from the Western Hemisphere idea by more urgent matters, such as the sharpening controversies of the United States with Britain and France over neutral rights and then the War of 1812. But interest in the application of the idea remained alive both in official circles and among the public at large, and during the postwar years it gained strength from the interaction of two new factors in the world situation. One of these was the growing threat from Europe through the "Holy Alliance." The other was the rise of the Latin American independence movement under regimes whose political orientation, whether republican, as in most cases, or monarchical, was of the same general revolutionary and liberal type as that represented by the United States and combatted by the "allied despots of Europe." [12]

The combined effect of these new factors was to sharpen the differentiation between the European and the American systems and to strengthen the foundations of the latter by adding mutuality of defense interests and ideology to the original concepts of New World and geographical unity. This was their combined effect in the United States, at any rate, and Henry Clay is a personal symbol of the process. He was the first leading statesman to sound the tocsin against the Holy Alliance, as he did in 1815 on his return from the ne-

[12] This and the next five paragraphs summarize the much more detailed discussion in Whitaker, *Independence*.

31

gotiation of the Treaty of Ghent with Great Britain. Five years later he also took the lead in proposing to meet this growing menace by the creation of a "system of which we shall be the centre, and in which all South America will act with us" in promoting inter-American commerce and at the same time establishing "the rallying point of human wisdom against all the despotism of the Old World." Or, as he put it the following year (1821) in a notable address at Lexington, Kentucky, "a sort of counterprise to the holy alliance should be formed in the two Americas, in favor of national independence and liberty."

By no means all of Clay's fellow countrymen shared his vision of America. Thus, the vitriolic John Randolph of Roanoke said in 1816: "The struggle for liberty in South America will turn out in the end something like the French liberty, a detestable despotism. You cannot make liberty out of Spanish matter—you might as well try to build a seventy-four out of pine saplings." Likewise, in 1821 Edward Everett, editor of the *North American Review,* warned its readers:

We have no concern with South America, . . . we can have no well founded sympathy with them [the South Americans]. We are sprung from different stocks, we speak different languages, we have been brought up in different social and moral schools, we have been governed by different codes of law, we profess radically different codes of religion. . . . Not all the treaties we could make, nor the commissioners we could send out, nor the money we could lend them, would transform their Pueyrredons and their Artigases, into Adamses or Franklins, or their Bolivars into Washingtons.

This common-sense skepticism was shared by many of Everett's countrymen, including one of the Adamses, the Secretary of State at that time. Yet about this time many of the skeptics, again including Secretary Adams, were converted to the new faith through the contagion of hemispheric mysticism. Everett himself admitted in the article just cited

32

that the policy based upon it, which he condemned, was being "powerfully supported." Support for the underlying idea of inter-American unity had, in fact, been on the increase ever since 1815, though opinions differed as to the form the unity should take. One form was indicated by Spanish Minister Onís' warning, sent to his government from Washington early in 1815, that many people in the United States were dreaming of "a universal republic of the Americas." With variations, this dream was embodied in two plans sketched at this time. One was the work of the British-born William Thornton, United States Commissioner of Patents, who, having designed the national capitol at Washington, now designed a federal union for the Americas under what he called a "Columbian, Incal or Supreme Government." The other came from the pen of former congressman Matthew Lyon, who assured James Monroe (Secretary of State at this time) that the Caribbean area was already prepared to enter into a federal union of the Americas, which would ultimately extend to Cape Horn and "give peace to the world."

More representative of North American practicality, however, was the pamphlet *South America*, published in 1817, by Henry M. Brackenridge, a writer of some note in his day and a close student of Spanish American affairs. His pamphlet clearly stated both of the component parts of the American system concept: first, the severance of America from Europe, and second, co-operation among the American states. But he disavowed the "visionary" idea of a great American congress at Panama and advocated not the federal union of the American nations but international co-operation among them.

Space permits us to give only one other example of the widespread expression of the Western Hemisphere idea in the United States at this early period. This one possesses special interest because it started a chain reaction which,

33

over a period of five years, spread from Washington to Paris and back again to Washington where, it has been claimed, it introduced a French influence into the formulation of the Monroe Doctrine. The chain began in 1818 with the publication in a Washington newspaper of an editorial complaining of the hostility of the Holy Alliance to "the commercial prosperity of America," pointing out "the advantages offered our commerce with the republics of South America" and urging that the United States make the most of these advantages by "adopting a policy purely American." There was nothing novel or otherwise remarkable about this editorial, but it was picked up and reproduced six weeks later in the Paris *Moniteur Universel*, from which the indefatigable French publicist Abbé de Pradt borrowed it to develop the prediction of an American system contained in his book, *L'Europe après le Congrès d'Aix la Chapelle*, published in 1819.

An English translation of this book was read by Thomas Jefferson in 1820, and it has been argued that it brought to full fruition the idea of the American system which Jefferson communicated to President Monroe in a letter of October 1823 and which the latter incorporated in his Doctrine the following December.[13] Actually, as we have seen, Jefferson's idea of the American system was already fully developed by 1813, and the importance of this part of Abbé de Pradt's book of 1819 lies rather in its influence in Latin America, where his reputation was greater than in the United States and where the idea of an all-American, and exclusively American, system was much less familiar.

Monroe, Adams, and the Farewell Address

The Western Hemisphere idea as expressed in the American system was first developed in the United States and was well known and widely supported there by the time that President

[13] For a citation and rebuttal, see the article by Bornholdt, *op. cit.*

Monroe made it the basis of a national policy in 1823. But, at least by implication, it conflicted with the even older and more deeply rooted United States policy of isolationism and could not flourish until the conflict had been resolved. This synthesis was worked out in two stages, the first of which is represented by the Monroe Doctrine and the second by President John Quincy Adams' message of March 1826 on the Panama Congress. Since Adams was the only leading participant in both stages, we cannot do better than follow the evolution of his thought as our main thread.[14]

With Adams, the first stage had its beginning either during or shortly before the drafting of the Monroe Doctrine. Certainly, at least as late as July 4, 1821, he was an unqualified isolationist,[15] and, like Everett of the *North American Review*, he scoffed at the whole idea of a continental American system. With regard to the latter he still held the views that he had so trenchantly expressed in 1820: "As to an American system, we [the United States] have it—we constitute the whole of it," and "there is no community of interests between North and South America . . . no basis for any such system." Adams' isolationism was rooted in Washington's Farewell Address of 1796; and, when squarely confronted with the question whether that policy, which Washington had declared with reference to Europe, should be extended to the new states of Latin America, the answer given in his Independence Day address in 1821 was a resounding "yes!" Moreover, he advocated giving the policy the same rigorous interpretation, so that it would not only prevent the formation of permanent "political entanglements" with the new states but,

---

[14] Except as otherwise noted, the rest of this chapter is based on Whitaker, *Independence*.

[15] In a recent notable work, Bemis refers to Adams as "the greatest isolationist of them all" (Samuel F. Bemis, *John Quincy Adams and the Foundations of American Foreign Policy* [New York, 1949], p. 553; cited hereafter as *John Quincy Adams*).

on the analogy of the United States' refusal to help the French Republic in its fight for life in the 1790's, it would also interdict United States military aid to the Latin American states for any purpose whatever, including even the defense of their independence against the Holy Alliance.

It required no little suppleness for the exponent of these views to reconcile himself less than a year and a half later to those parts of the Monroe Doctrine which for the first time based United States foreign policy upon the concept of the American system and made a startling application of the new policy by warning the European powers not to interfere with or oppress the new states of Latin America in any way, with the clear implication of a resort to arms in case the warning should not be heeded. How Adams reconciled himself to all this is suggested by the account given in his diary of the cabinet discussions from which the Doctrine emerged. This account indicates that he accepted the American system and its corollary, the warning to Europe, as the lesser of two evils, that is to say, as the only alternative to an even more far-reaching departure from isolationism which President Monroe seemed disposed to make in accordance with advice given by former Presidents Jefferson and Madison. This departure might take one or both of two forms: either acceptance of British Foreign Secretary George Canning's proposal of a joint declaration by Britain and the United States on behalf of Spanish America, as Jefferson advised, or the broadening of the declaration to include Greece and Spain as well as Spanish America, as Madison advised. In both cases the effect would have been to strike at the very core of the isolationist policy, which was isolation from Europe.

To avoid this greater evil, Adams accepted the lesser one represented by the American system. Indeed, since the mood of his chief, the President, left him no alternative, he not only accepted but championed an idea and a policy of which until so recently he had never had a good word to say.

To be sure, Adams cloaked his conversion to the Western Hemisphere idea with the mantle of nationalism and justified the assumption by the United States of the defense of the whole Hemisphere on the ground that the designs of the Holy Alliance upon the New World *might* include an effort by France to recover Louisiana, with the result that, as he put. it, "the danger . . . was brought to our own doors, and I thought we could not too soon take our stand to repel it." But this explanation did not alter the fact that the means chosen to repel the danger was the assertion of a doctrine of Hemisphere defense which applied to remote Chile and Argentina as well as to adjacent Mexico and to a whole group of countries with which, whether remote or nearby, the United States had, according to the Adams of 1820, "no community of interests." In other words, while he still clung to isolationism where Europe was concerned, he made a long retreat from it in the case of Latin America, and since the latter included countries so remote or alien that the retreat could not be justified on rational grounds, one can only conclude that Adams was falling under the sway of the mystique of Pan Americanism which had been foreshadowed in Jefferson's Humboldt letter of 1813.

To be sure, Adams did not at once go on to develop the positive implications of the American system; nor, for that matter, did President Monroe or anyone else in the administration do so. None of the new states was consulted while the new Doctrine was being drawn up; and, after it had been announced, no effort was made to obtain their support or co-operation in enforcing it. On the contrary, the efforts that some of the new states themselves made in that direction were uniformly rejected in the remaining year of Monroe's presidency and generally discouraged in Adams' four-year administration which followed it. In fact, it was in these years that the United States government defined the Doctrine in the terms to which it inflexibly adhered for more than a century to come, namely, as a unilateral national policy of the United States and therefore not an appropriate subject for inter-American action.

Nevertheless, it is abundantly clear that Adams, while President, did make another retreat away from isolationism and in the direction of inter-American co-operation. He was doubtless encouraged to do so by his Secretary of State, Henry Clay, one of the earliest and most ardent advocates of the American system. Nowhere was Adams' new concept of hemispheric relations set forth more clearly than in the message of March 15, 1826, to the lower house of Congress,[16] explaining why he wanted the United States to participate in the Panama Congress, which was now at last about to meet for defense against European aggression and other purposes.[17] After discussing these purposes, Adams squarely confronted the question of "whether," as he put it, "the measure might not have a tendency to change the policy, hitherto invariably pursued by the United States, of avoiding all entangling alliances and all unnecessary foreign connections." In other words, did it conflict with the "great rule" of isolationism set forth in Washington's Farewell Address? His answer was an emphatic "No!" On the contrary, he declared, "The acceptance of this invitation . . . far from conflicting with the counsel or the policy of Washington, is directly deducible from and conformable to it."

The basic assumption of his answer was that "the counsel of Washington . . . like all the counsels of wisdom, was founded upon the circumstances in which our country and the

16 Richardson, *op. cit.*, II, 329–340.
17 For a recent discussion of this subject, see Bemis, *John Quincy Adams,* ch. xxvi, "President Adams, Henry Clay, and Latin America."

world around us were situated at the time when it was given [1796]." Now, thirty years later, the circumstances were still substantially the same as regarded Europe; so that, Adams implied, isolationism should still be the United States' policy toward Europe. But as regarded Latin America, the situation was quite otherwise. In the interval, he said, "A political hurricane has gone over three fourths of the civilized portions of the earth . . . leaving at least the American atmosphere purified and refreshed," with the former European colonies now "transformed into eight independent nations . . . seven of them republics like ourselves," while our own "population, our wealth, our territorial extension, our power —physical and moral—have nearly trebled." Without pausing to explain the nice calculation by which he had ascertained that the moral power of the United States had *nearly* trebled, Adams marched on to his triumphant conclusion. This he stated in the form of a rhetorical question:

Reasoning upon this state of things from the sound and judicious principles of Washington, must we not say that the period which he predicted . . . has arrived, that *America* has a set of primary interests which have none or a remote relation to Europe; that . . . if she [Europe] should interfere [in America] as she may . . . we might be called in defence of our own altars and firesides to take an attitude which would cause our neutrality to be respected and choose peace or war, as our interest, guided by justice, should counsel.

He then fortified this conclusion by quoting the American-system, warning-to-Europe portions of the Monroe Doctrine.[18] These did, in fact, support his present position, but the

18 That Adams, of all people, should have done this seems to me to require extensive modification of the statement made by Perkins in the first of his magistral studies of the Monroe Doctrine, that "in 1825 there was no doctrinaire attachment to the dogma of the complete separation of the New World from the Old" (Dexter Perkins, *The Monroe Doctrine, 1823–1826* [Cambridge, 1932], p. 204).

latter was more advanced than the one that he and his chief, Monroe, had taken in the Doctrine of 1823. Adams now gave the idea of the American system a further extension by adding the element of international co-operation among the states composing that system—including, specifically, co-operation in support of the noncolonization part of the Doctrine. This is something which Monroe had neither suggested in his Doctrine nor sought to achieve in practice.

To be sure, the scope of inter-American co-operation as Adams envisaged it seems narrow by present-day standards, for he stipulated, among other things, that the Panama Congress would be merely consultative so far as the United States was concerned; but the standards by which we should measure his policy are those of his own day. According to these, he made a great contribution to the growth of the American system as the political expression of the Western Hemisphere idea; and in so doing he provided the best justification for the paradoxical saying of the twentieth-century Chilean scholar Alejandro Alvarez that the roots of multilateral Pan Americanism lie in the unilateral Monroe Doctrine.

Yet, however contradictorily, Adams had also contrived to represent his embryonic Pan Americanism as a projection of the isolationist policy of the Farewell Address. In doing so, he struck a prophetic, or, if one prefers, an ominous note. It was to be struck again and again in later years, perhaps never more strongly than in the 1930's—with the dire results for the Western Hemisphere idea that will be noted in their proper place.

III

Divided America

THE Panama Congress of 1826 represented the convergence of two ideas whose meeting promised for a brief moment to prove a fruitful union. The first of these, which came from the United States, was the idea of the unity of the Western Hemisphere nations in some rather vague and undefined way. Spanish America then contributed the other idea, which was that of rendering this hemispheric fraternity more effective by international co-operation of a politico-military character, whether through a league, a confederation, or otherwise.

Fiasco after Panama

As it turned out, the marriage of the two Americas ended in divorce before there was even a honeymoon. At Panama, Uncle Sam left the Spanish American bride waiting at the church. In Mexico the following year, the scene was re-enacted, but with the roles reversed: this time it was Uncle Sam who lingered at the altar in vain. After that, the unhappy couple drifted further and further apart for nearly

41

forty years; it is with the story of their estrangement that the present essay deals.

The basic reason for this sad state of affairs seems quite clear. It was the result of an effort to unite two movements that were then incompatible, and the effort only led to frustration for both. The internationalism of Spanish America was the outgrowth of an effort to form an exclusively Spanish American union on the analogy of the formation of the United States out of the former English colonies, and that effort was only handicapped (as the Anglo-American effort would have been) when to its original limited objective was added the overambitious one of uniting the whole Hemisphere. The Hemisphere idea, in turn, suffered from becoming identified almost at the outset with the politico-military type of internationalism advocated for their own special purposes by the leaders of the Spanish American movement.

The story to be told in this essay is therefore not one of success, but the very vicissitudes through which the Western Hemisphere idea passed make it an instructive one for the student of the history of that idea. Since a large part of the story was prefigured in the fiasco of Panama, it is important to consider how and why that meeting failed so dismally to fulfill its promise.[1]

The question how—that is, in what respect and to what extent—the Congress failed is best approached by first noting how it succeeded. The Congress lasted three weeks in June and July of 1826, and was attended by delegates from Mexico, Central America, Greater Colombia, and Peru, and by an official British observer and an unofficial Dutch observer. The United States was not represented; it appointed two delegates, but their appointment was delayed so long by

[1] For accounts of the Panama Congress in English, with citations of sources and secondary accounts in Spanish as well as English, see Bemis, *John Quincy Adams,* pp. 543–565, and Whitaker, *Independence,* pp. 564–584.

partisan opposition (of which more later) that neither of them reached Panama. Perhaps the greatest success of the Congress lay in the fact that it took place at all, for it was the first international conference ever held in America. Also, it brought together delegates from several American countries and, once assembled, they achieved enough to render the meeting a notable precedent for future generations. Though only four Spanish American countries were represented, they embraced an area occupied by eleven of the present twenty states of Latin America. This large area extended continuously from California down through Peru, and at that time it contained three fourths of the population of Spanish America.

The principal achievements of the Congress were two. First, it adopted a number of treaties providing for broad multilateral co-operation, in defense and other matters, which anticipated a large part of what was to be accomplished by subsequent inter-American conferences down to our own day. Second, it provided for the resumption of its labors at another congress to be held at Tacubaya, Mexico, the following year, and thus established at the outset the principle of the continuity of inter-American co-operation.

Though all this adds up to a substantial degree of success, the Panama Congress has gone down in history as a failure. That judgment is correct only if the term "Panama Congress" is used in a broad sense to mean not only the Congress itself but also its sequel. It is in this broad sense that we have spoken of the Panama fiasco, for the failure came after the Congress adjourned. The fiasco was twofold, consisting first, in the failure of all the governments concerned, except the Colombian, to ratify the Panama agreements, with the result that these remained a dead letter; and second, in the failure of the follow-up congress to meet at Tacubaya, Mexico, the next year, as stipulated at Panama. The disillusionment of this double failure increased the already widespread opposi-

43

tion to the hemispheric movement, which was brought to a full stop by two simultaneous developments: the subsidence of the threat from the Holy Alliance and the outbreak in Spanish America of what Pedro Henríquez-Ureña calls "the latent anarchy of the colonial regime," in the form of an alternation of civil war and despotism that was to scourge most of Spanish America for a generation or more to come.

As a result, Bolívar and most other internationalists in the new states reverted to their earlier idea of an exclusively Spanish American, or at most Latin American, association of nations; some, including Bolívar himself, went even further and ended as isolationists. Likewise, public opinion in the United States reverted so far toward a simon-pure isolationism that, for years to come, the Monroe Doctrine was almost forgotten even as a strictly unilateral, national policy; as for its multilateral, Pan American implications, these were completely forgotten. The story accordingly bifurcates at this point, and its main thread must be followed first in one of the Americas and then in the other.

Jacksonians, isolation, and Manifest Destiny

In order to understand the situation that developed in the United States after the Panama Congress, we must first go back to the great debate over the question of whether the United States should participate in it. The debate was waged both in Congress and by the public at large, but this essay is concerned with only the Congressional phase of it. This was focused upon the message of March 1826, quoted in the preceding essay, in which President Adams stated his new policy of international co-operation with the Latin American states, argued that it was in fact merely a new application of policies already set forth in Washington's Farewell Address and the Monroe Doctrine, and sought the support of the legislative branch for his decision to implement the new policy by sending delegates to the Panama Congress. At this time the weight of public opinion was probably on Adams' side, though the generally well-informed Jared Sparks, editor of the *North American Review,* was doubtless guilty of great exaggeration when he wrote that "the mission to Panama was universally popular among the people." At any rate, we have no reason to believe that opinion in the United States Congress of that day was totally unlike public opinion at large, and in Congress the "mission to Panama" met with formidable opposition.

This opposition came mainly from four sources: party politics, the slaveholding South, economic interests, and the isolationist tradition. The most important of these was party politics. Adams had won the bitterly contested presidential election of 1824–1825 by a narrow margin over Andrew Jackson, whose supporters, with an eye on the next presidential election, that of 1828, kept up a running fight against Adams throughout his administration in the hope of discrediting him by defeating whatever measures he proposed. The Panama mission was made to order for their purposes, for it enabled them to fuse and harden all these opposition elements by adding the amalgam of an isolationism bearing the label of the great George Washington. They complained that Adams had caught the "Spanish American fever" from Clay, and they flatly denied Adams' claim that his new Latin American policy was a true corollary of the rule laid down in the Farewell Address. They clamored, through one of their chief spokesmen, James Buchanan of Pennsylvania, for the defeat of the Panama mission and a return to the "policy of Washington," which they defined as "independence of all foreign nations." [2]

[2] *Register of Debates in Congress,* 19th Cong., 1st Sess., 1826, pp. 2175, 2182. For a broad discussion of isolation, see Albert K. Weinberg, "The Historical Meaning of the Doctrine of Isolation," *American Political Science Review,* XXXIV (1940), 542 ff.

Though they failed in their effort to defeat the mission, they did muster enough opposition to delay it so long that, as we have seen, the United States delegates never reached Panama. One of them, the minister to Colombia, died on his way to the Congress; the other, John Sergeant, a prominent Philadelphia lawyer, did not even start for Panama. He did, however, go to Mexico to take part in the second phase of the inter-American congress, at Tacubaya; and he and his fellow-delegate, the resident minister, Joel Roberts Poinsett, an ardent Pan Americanist, prepared eagerly for what they hoped would be an epoch-making international conference, in which the United States would seize the opportunity, lost at Panama, to put itself at the head of a hemispheric association of nations.

Once again fortune favored the Jacksonian isolationists, for the projected Tacubaya congress never met. After cooling his heels in highland Mexico City for several months, Sergeant packed up his papers and went home, leaving Poinsett to carry on his Pan American projects as best he could through the regular diplomatic channels of the Mexico City legation. As it turned out, Poinsett's best was not good enough, and it was not until more than sixty years later that representatives of the United States and its sister republics of the Western Hemisphere sat down together in an international conference.

For the United States, the long-range significance of the Panama-Tacubaya fiasco lies in three facts: first, that in the course of it the Jacksonian party took an isolationist position which excluded co-operation with Latin America; second, that its choice seemed to be validated by the subsequent failure of all Spanish American efforts to salvage the inter-American movement; and third, that this same Jacksonian party (soon to take the name Democratic) was normally in control of the United States government for the next third of a century, which stretched from the end of the unfortunate Adams administration in 1829 (Jackson did defeat him, as planned) to the outbreak of the Civil War in the United States in 1861. The general orientation of the Democratic party's foreign policy during this long period is indicated by the fact that one of its chief spokesmen in this field was the James Buchanan mentioned above as an extreme isolationist and opponent of the Panama mission. In this period Buchanan was minister to Russia and Britain, Secretary of State, and, finally, President of the United States.

Under these circumstances the Western Hemisphere idea could not prosper. Inter-American co-operation was not seriously considered even when it was suggested by Latin American governments, as happened occasionally. The effective scope of the Monroe Doctrine itself was reduced from hemisphere to quarter-sphere proportions by President Polk's new "doctrine" of 1845, which implied that the United States' mantle of protection now covered only North America. His Secretary of State at this time was our old friend James Buchanan.

One of the main reasons for this narrowing of the United States' outlook was its preoccupation with the fulfillment of its Manifest Destiny by extending its national domain westward on a broad front all the way to the Pacific Ocean.[3] The extension was achieved mainly through the vast territorial acquisitions of the 1840's—Texas, Oregon, New Mexico, California—and mainly at the expense of Mexico; but the expansionist theme was dominant over a much longer period, embraced a much wider range of territories, and included other objectives besides direct territorial acquisition. Its dominance began within a few years after the Panama fiasco and continued down to the outbreak of the Civil War in 1861. In addition to the territories actually acquired, it looked to the

[3] Weinberg, *Manifest Destiny:* pp. 100–129 and *passim* (cf. index).

47

acquisition of Cuba and part or all of Mexico and Central America. It took such other forms in addition to outright annexation as President Buchanan's proposal to establish a United States protectorate over Mexico (which might be regarded as an alternative to annexation) and the treaty of 1846 with New Granada (Colombia), by which the United States acquired important transit rights in Panama in return for guaranteeing Colombia's sovereignty over the Isthmus— the only such guarantee the United States made to any country in the nineteenth century.[4]

So far we have been concerned with the Jacksonian Democrats, but much the same could be said of the other national party of this period, the Whig. It was less aggressively expansionist, but equally nationalist, isolationist, and forgetful of the hemispheric vision of the preceding generation. Thus it was that in 1852 a Whig Secretary of State, Edward Everett, could discuss the international status of Cuba without reference to Spanish American interest in it and that in 1862 Lincoln's Secretary of State, William H. Seward, a former Whig, evaded participation in a projected inter-American conference, similar to the Panama Congress of 1826, which was soon to be held in Lima, Peru.

New leadership: Mexico and Peru

The conference in question belongs to the Latin American part of the story. Colombia's leadership in the inter-American movement came to an end with the Panama fiasco, partly because Bolívar was so disillusioned by it that he lost interest in the effort to form a general American confederation or league. For a time he shifted his attention to the smaller but still ambitious plan for a Federation of the Andes, a kind of super-

[4] Samuel F. Bemis, *The Latin American Policy of the United States: An Historical Interpretation* (New York, 1943), pp. 73–97. Cited hereafter as *Latin American Policy*.

state which he hoped would extend from Mexico to Chile. Then, disappointed again, he swung to the opposite extreme of isolationist Colombian nationalism. The little-noticed document in which this about-face is recorded forms a rather startling epilogue to the story that began with the internationalist Jamaica Letter of 1815. The document in question is a note of August 14, 1828, written by order of Bolívar, instructing Colombian minister Pedro Gual to break off his mission to Mexico. The note reads:

The decision of His Excellency [Bolívar] has been very carefully considered and is irrevocable. He agrees with you that, for the present, Colombia ought to devote itself entirely to its own affairs, think of its own interests, endeavor to establish itself firmly both at home and in its relations with the European powers from which it can hope for the best advantages, and abandon intervention in the common affairs of the American states.[5]

In 1829 Bolívar carried his new policy to the extreme of seeking a separate peace for Colombia with Spain.[6]

Posterity has almost invariably ignored Bolívar's rather dreary ending in isolationism and has pictured him only as the author of the Jamaica Letter and the Panama Congress. Oddly enough, his own contemporaries seem to have done likewise. Whatever the explanation of the latter fact may be, it is an important one for our story, for in the next decade after Bolívar's death, the government of Colombia was in the hands of men who had opposed him in his lifetime and who now continued to oppose all his works, one of the most characteristic of which, they thought, was the inter-American movement. Hence it was partly by default that in the next generation the leadership of this movement passed from Bolívar's own country to Mexico and Peru. Yet the leadership might have been lost even if there had been no default, for in 1830

[5] Cavelier, *op. cit.,* p. 84.   [6] Bierck, *op. cit.,* p. 540.

Greater Colombia broke up into three separate states, Venezuela, New Granada (the present Colombia), and Ecuador, and none of these succession states had the prestige or power necessary to maintain such a position.

The mantle fell first upon Mexico, which from 1831 to 1842 made five separate efforts to assemble a Spanish American congress and on the last occasion sent a special envoy on a tour to whip up interest in the project. All five of these efforts failed, but their failure is of interest because it paved the way for an ultimate return to the Western Hemisphere idea by showing that the narrower idea of Spanish American unity did not provide the integrating principle necessary for effective international co-operation. Despite the existence of a common cultural heritage, in political and economic matters Spanish American unity was the most transparent of fictions. As we shall see, Argentina was to urge this objection forcefully and effectively in the 1860's.

Mexico sought to fortify Spanish American unity by introducing a new element—Yankeephobia; but this aroused little response until too late to do the Mexicans any good. Even in countries bordering on the Caribbean, fear of the United States had not yet become sufficiently strong to serve as cement for such a union. Thus, New Granada did not even reply to the first four Mexican invitations, in the 1830's; Venezuela flatly rejected the fifth, in 1842; and as late as 1846 New Granada chose to base the defense of its precious Panama territory upon a bilateral alliance with the United States itself. By this time Yankeephobia had begun to spread to other parts of Spanish America; but the very events that brought this about—the United States' annexation of Texas in 1845 and its war with Mexico in 1846, which ended in its acquisition of New Mexico and California in 1848—so weakened Mexico as to destroy any possibility of effective international leadership by the latter.

Peru, which supplanted Mexico in the mid-40's and held the lead for the next two decades, promptly brought the inter-American movement back into line with the Panama precedent by restoring its broad hemispheric character and by making its primary purpose once again defense against aggression from Europe, not from the United States. Several circumstances combined to make Peru's leadership more successful than Mexico's had been. Peru occupied a more central geographical position in Spanish America; during these two decades it was politically more stable and orderly, and enjoyed greater prosperity, thanks largely to the growth of the new guano industry; and its foreign office was headed by a succession of exceptionally able ministers. Last but not least, it was an advantage to the Peruvians' broader movement that they linked it explicitly to the Bolivarian tradition, for with the passage of time a sentimental aura had gathered about this tradition. Personal rancor against the dead hero Bolívar had subsided in New Granada, which now broke out of its isolationist shell of the 1830's and collaborated wholeheartedly with Peru in the latter's effort to revive the Bolivarian tradition and translate it into action.

Its revival was made easier by the reappearance at this time of the same type of threat from Europe which had produced the inter-American movement in the first place. The threat now took the form, not of a new Holy Alliance, but of a military expedition which was being openly organized in England in September 1846 by an exiled Ecuadorian *político,* General Juan José Flores, with support in Spain and elsewhere on the Continent, supposedly for the purpose of setting up a monarchy which would embrace most of northern South America. While the South American diplomats in London protested to Lord Palmerston (who, after some delay, heeded their protests and scotched the expedition), their home governments prepared defense measures, both collectively and individually. Peru took the lead in collective defense, and it was encouraged to do so by the fact that in 1839 the Peruvian Constituent Assembly had unanimously approved a proposal that Peru invite the "Hispanic American" republics to a "continental congress" to provide for defense against "foreign aggression" and other purposes.[7]

Accordingly, as soon as the warning of Flores' expedition reached Lima from the Peruvian envoy in London, Foreign Minister Paz Soldán hurriedly dispatched (on November 9, 1846) invitations to a continental congress of plenipotentiaries to be held in Lima in defense of the "American cause." The immediate objective was described as being the security of South America, but that was because that was the only part of America which was immediately threatened from Europe. With this exception, both the invitation and the accompanying note stressed the continent-wide character of the proposed congress. The circular invitation was sent not only to the Spanish American states, from Mexico to Chile and Argentina, but also to Brazil and the United States; it described the congress as an effort to realize the purposes of the Panama Congress; and the accompanying note contained many such phrases as "the governments of America," "the peoples of the American continent," "the American republics," and "American rights"—not once was the narrower term "Spanish American" used in this context.[8]

Except for the United States, which was not only still in the midst of its isolationist reaction but was also embroiled in a war with Mexico, the response to Peru's invitation ranged from warm to enthusiastic. The general idea of continental co-operation was applauded even by normally isolationist Argentina and monarchical Brazil, though the latter, for obvi-

[7] Alberto Ulloa, *Congresos americanos de Lima* (Lima, 1938), I, pp. lv–lviii. In his long and learned Prólogo, pp. iii–clxxxvii, Ulloa cites the documents which make up the rest of these two volumes.

[8] *Ibid.*, I, p. xxx.

ous reasons, qualified its endorsement insofar as the term
"American *republics*" was concerned. Argentina went so far
as to promise its "most efficacious co-operation" in meeting
aggression, wherever it might occur, "with as much determination as if the territory of Argentina itself were attacked."

The results achieved after all this fanfare seem at first sight
quite disappointing. The congress was actually held at Lima
(December 1847–February 1848), but only the five west coast
republics of South America took part in it, and, as in the
case of the Panama Congress, not one of the treaties adopted
by it was subsequently carried out or even ratified. The at-
tendance was not only small but also exclusively Spanish
American, with the result that the Lima Congress had to
operate within a Spanish American framework.

Nevertheless, the Congress is important because it did
something to promote the Western Hemisphere idea and still
more to clarify the problem of its political application. Though
it addressed itself primarily to Spanish America, its principal
pacts, the treaties of Confederation and of Commerce and
Navigation (February 1848), were expressly left open to
adherence by all the American governments, with the stipula-
tion that they should all not only be permitted but urged to
adhere. Symbolically, the Treaty of Confederation provided
that its seal should be a hemisphere showing "the American
continent," and bearing around the border the words "American Confederation." [9] In the circumstances, this was about
all the Congress could have done to promote the Western
Hemisphere idea. Coming on top of the preconference discussion in the same sense, which we have already noted, it
helped to keep this idea from being permanently supplanted
in Spanish America by the rival concept of an exclusively
Spanish American union.

The problem of the political application of this idea was

[9] *Ibid.*, I, 309–310, Article 19 of the treaty.

clarified in two closely related ways. In the first place, the term "confederation" had been used rather vaguely and loosely by Bolívar and others to indicate the form that American unity should take, thereby conjuring up visions of a superstate which antagonized many people in Latin America as well as the United States. The Lima Congress did much to allay opposition on this ground. It still used the term confederation but took the sting out of it by making it clear that what was intended was not a true confederation but a league of nations with precisely defined and rather narrowly limited powers for the two purposes of defense against aggression by a non-American power and the peaceful settlement of international disputes among the members. In the second place, the national sovereignty of each of the member states was stipulated and protected. The Treaty of Confederation established what in modern parlance is called a nonaggression pact, but at the same time it established the rule of absolute nonintervention among the states. The rule in question was adopted after the Congress had rejected a Bolivian proposal of an opposite intent, namely, that the member states should intervene to support constitutional governments against revolution.

In this connection mention should be made of a fact which has an important bearing upon the content of the Western Hemisphere idea. This is the fact that, beginning with Bolívar, intervention has had many advocates in Latin America, though on different and sometimes conflicting grounds. In the decade before the Lima Congress, two of its advocates, Pedro Felix Vicuña and Juan Bautista Alberdi, made proposals that anticipated the most notable expression of interventionism in our own day, the Rodríguez Larreta Doctrine of 1945, which proposed multilateral intervention in defense of human rights and democracy. In 1837 Vicuña, a Chilean, published a pamphlet in which he argued that the General

Congress of America, which he envisaged, ought to support popular revolutions against tyrannical governments. In 1844 Alberdi, one of the Argentine refugees in Chile from the tyranny of Rosas, maintained that intervention should promote the general economic and social welfare of the American states.[10] While the anti-interventionists prevailed, both in that early period and later, they did not silence the other side, and the pros and cons of intervention have continued to form one of the chief themes of the inter-American movement to the present day.

During the period of Peruvian leadership, two other international events—the adoption of the Continental Treaty of 1856, and the second Congress of Lima, 1864–1865—illustrate two widely divergent tendencies in the development of the Hemisphere idea and its application.

The Continental Treaty was signed at Santiago, Chile, in September 1856 by the representatives of Chile, Peru, and Ecuador.[11] Though never ratified, it is noteworthy for two reasons. In the first place, though it invoked the precedent of Panama, it not only excluded but was aimed against the United States, whose expansion at the expense of Mexico and whose filibustering at the expense of Nicaragua had aroused widespread apprehension in Latin America by this time. Moreover, while the republican United States was excluded, monarchical Brazil was urged to adhere. Thus the Continental Treaty represents the perversion of the Western Hemisphere idea to the purpose of uniting one portion of the Hemisphere against another—Latin America against the United States. In doing so, it weakened one article of the hemispheric faith

[10] Robert N. Burr and Roland D. Hussey, eds., *Documents on Inter-American Cooperation, 1810–1881* [Philadelphia, 1955], docs. no. 19 (Vicuna) and no. 23 (Alberdi).

[11] Gustave A. Nuermberger, "The Continental Treaties of 1856," *Hispanic American Historical Review*, XX (1940), 32–55; and Ulloa, *op. cit.*, I, pp. xc–xcvi, xcix–cii.

(defense against Europe) and eliminated another (the affinity of common republican institutions).

In the second place, the Continental Treaty reversed the pattern of both the Panama Congress and the first Lima Congress by stressing nonpolitical rather than political objectives. Its text deals first with nonpolitical matters of common concern, such as contracts, coastwise shipping, postal service, and domestic law, and only then moves on, by a sort of process of deduction (as Alberto Ulloa puts it), to build up political principles and duties on the basis thus laid. This was done mainly because the practicability of the politico-military approach was beginning to be seriously doubted but partly also because European aggression (always the main incentive to politico-military union in America) was not threatening at that time. The doubts continued to multiply through the years; and when, a generation later, the United States rejoined Latin America in the inter-American movement, the predominantly nonpolitical pattern first established by this Continental Treaty was followed more closely than any other during the first forty years of Pan American co-operation.

Turning point: The second Lima Congress

Without entirely abandoning the new pattern, the second Lima Congress, held eight years later, shifted the emphasis back again to political union and military defense for the very good reason that the menace from Europe had by this time emerged again and was indeed even more serious than in the days of the Holy Alliance. The armies of Napoleon III had overrun most of Mexico and had set up a puppet empire there under the Hapsburg Archduke Maximilian; Spain had recolonized Santo Domingo; and Spanish warships had seized Peru's Chincha Islands (an important source of its valuable guano trade) and were threatening like aggression against continental Peru. Moreover, the United States was immobilized by a civil war which had encouraged these aggressions, and Great Britain had done nothing to prevent them.

The Congress was held in Lima from December 1864 to March 1865 and adopted four treaties, of which the most important was the Treaty of Union and Defensive Alliance.[12] The treaties were of the kind long since made familiar: they were linked to the politico-military tradition of the Congress of Panama, and they breathed the spirit of continental solidarity. But again not one of them was ratified; even before the Congress adjourned there were many indications that the line they were following led into a blind alley. Despite the gravity of the crisis, it was possible to bring together fully accredited representatives from only seven states (Bolivia, Chile, El Salvador, Colombia, Ecuador, Venezuela, and Peru). Argentina was represented, informally and against its will, by the already famous Domingo Faustino Sarmiento, who was hamstrung by his government's settled opposition to the whole concept of a politico-military league of the Americas. In the opinion of Argentine President Mitre and Foreign Minister Elizalde, it was childish and pernicious nonsense to talk about the American nations as constituting a group of "sister states" set apart from and in opposition to Europe.[13] The truth is, said Elizalde, that "the American republics have more ties of common interest and sympathy with several of the European states than with one another." [14] On such

[12] Ulloa, *op. cit.*, I, pp. cv–cxxxix. Robert W. Frazer, "The Role of the Lima Congress, 1864–1865, in the Development of Pan Americanism," *Hispanic American Historical Review*, XXIX (1949), 319–348, brings together a great deal of interesting information, but fails to come to grips with the question implied in its title, or indeed to justify the use of the term "Pan Americanism" in this connection.

[13] Ricardo Rojas, *El profeta de la pampa: Vida de Sarmiento* (Buenos Aires, 1945), pp. 471–472.

[14] Ulloa, *op. cit.*, I, 646. This was stated in a note written by Elizalde in 1862, but he expressed the same idea almost as strongly in 1864. See Carlos Alberto Silva, ed., *La política internacional de la Argentina* (Buenos Aires, 1946), pp. 26–27.

grounds as these the government of Argentina had rejected the Continental Treaty of 1856, reaffirming that country's time-honored policy of bilateral alliances; and by the same reasoning, it reduced Sarmiento's status at Lima to that of a mere observer.

Even in the small group of full-fledged representatives at Lima there was much disagreement. Chile had from the start taken the strong continental line that no congress should be held to which all the American nations had not been invited, and the United States had been omitted from the guest list of this one. Sarmiento devoted his principal speech to urging the delegates to think more about cultural co-operation on the basis of reports he would send them annually about books and education in the United States (to which he was on his way as Argentine minister).[15] Some of the delegates objected to the anti-European tone of the whole inter-American movement; one of them, a Bolivian, arguing the interdependence and essential harmony of Europe and America, quoted an unnamed writer (*pensador*) to the effect that "God put the fever in Europe and the quinine in America in order to teach us the solidarity that should prevail among all the peoples of the earth." All the foreign delegates were irritated by the weakness toward Spain now shown by Peru, which had called the Congress primarily to concert resistance to Spanish aggression.

Outside the Congress—and most of America had remained outside of it—the situation was even worse. To mention only the two largest countries, Brazil had again failed to respond to the invitation to a congress, and as for the United States, everyone knew that it would not have taken part in the Congress even if it had been invited. Secretary Seward had made

[15] Joseph R. Barager, "Sarmiento and the United States," MS, doctoral dissertation, 1951, University of Pennsylvania Library. The account of this aspect of Sarmiento's career in Allison W. Bunkley, *The Life of Sarmiento* (Princeton, 1952), is rather sketchy.

that clear in 1862, and in doing so he was only adhering to the line followed by his predecessors in the State Department ever since the days of Adams and Clay. To growing numbers of Latin Americans, the aloofness of the United States was a source of gratification, since it saved them from the embarrassment of shutting the door in the face of an unwanted guest.

Indeed, the major trend of the period since 1845 had been toward a division of the Hemisphere into the two Americas and the appropriation of the Hemisphere idea to the exclusive use of one of them—Latin America. In the process, the idea was necessarily denatured. Its bedrock basis, which was geographical, was obviously abandoned when one of the largest states of the Hemisphere was excluded. Its political basis was undermined by the attempted inclusion of monarchical Brazil and the exclusion of the republican United States. And its original bias against Europe was being converted into a bias in favor of at least a part of Europe which was so pronounced that it found strong expression in some quarters (notably in Argentina and Bolivia) even at the height of the European aggressions unleashed during the Civil War of 1861–1865 in the United States. In short, the hemispheric idea was paradoxically being employed to expand Spanish Americanism into a Latin Americanism tending toward a *rapprochement* with Europe.

Further development along this line was impeded by the inner contradictions of the paradox and still more by the fact that the new Latin Americanism was tied to an older politico-military instrument, of which the Panama Congress was the archetype and which the experience of forty years had proved unworkable. The final proof came with the crowning fiasco of the second Lima Congress. It was the last congress of its kind ever held and its failure marks a turning point.[16] The

[16] In 1883 a Bolivarian Conference, with representatives of eight Spanish

way was now prepared for a fresh approach to the Hemisphere idea under new leadership.

American states, met at Caracas, Venezuela. Though it recommended the calling of a continental diplomatic conference for the purpose of giving more precise form to "the American Union," it concerned itself with such matters as arbitration and the *uti possidetis*. Yepes, a leading authority, regards this as "un signe avant-coureur des conférences panaméricaines" (Jesús M. Yepes, *La philosophie du Panaméricanisme* [Neuchâtel, 1945], p. 95).

IV ⚘

New Synthesis:

Sarmiento and Blaine

THE preceding essay described the divergence of thought that opened between the two Americas in the forty years following the fiasco of the Panama Congress of 1826. The present essay will show how, reversing this trend, fresh currency and a new interpretation were given to the Western Hemisphere idea in a period of equal length stretching from the collapse of the liberal revolutions of 1848 in Europe to the first Pan American conference, held at Washington in 1889–1890. Obviously, the two periods overlap; but sharply defined periods are at best an arbitrary device justified by convenience, and this device would do too much violence to the facts if applied to the complicated process under consideration.

This process was the result of the interplay of cultural and economic as well as political forces arising on both sides of the Atlantic. In the interest of clarity, and taking the calculated risk of oversimplification, the process will be described here in terms of two converging trends—first, the one symbolized by Domingo Faustino Sarmiento, writer, educator, diplomat, President of Argentina, and ardent admirer of the United States; and then a trend in the latter country symbolized by James Gillespie Blaine, twice Secretary of State, perennial presidential aspirant, and pioneer of Pan Americanism. In Latin America, the trend was away from the galloping Yankeephobia of the 1840's and 50's and toward a hemispheric view of inter-American solidarity and willingness to accept the leadership of the United States in making this view politically effective. In the United States, the trend was toward breaching the hard and fast isolationism of the pre-Civil War generation and toward the assumption of such leadership, though on different terms from those contemplated in the days of Monroe, Adams, and Clay.

Positivism

A philosophical vogue played an important part in first checking the estrangement between the two Americas and then bringing about a new *rapprochement* between them. This vogue was positivism, which enjoyed great popularity in Latin America in the second half of the nineteenth century, and above all in its last two decades. To be sure, there were considerable differences from country to country in the timing and intensity of the vogue as well as in the meaning given the term and in the relative influence of Auguste Comte and Herbert Spencer. Nevertheless, it is the opinion of the leading authority on the subject, Leopoldo Zea, that in Spanish America at large, no other philosophical current since the scholasticism that dominated the colonial era has equaled

positivism in importance.[1] Its importance for this study re-
sides in the fact that it was not confined to closet philosophers
but was widely applied to public policy and that its spread in
Latin America contributed—as the Enlightenment had done
for a time—to a better understanding with the United States
and thus to the reinvigoration of the Western Hemisphere
idea.

As Zea points out, positivism provided the Latin America
of the second generation of national independence with a
body of thought which it sorely needed and was well prepared to receive. The first generation had been characterized
by adherence to ideas of the eighteenth-century Enlightenment, particularly that of "enlightened despotism," but this
had led to the pattern of alternating dictatorships and civil
war of which we have already spoken and to widespread disillusionment and a quest for something better adapted to the
American scene. The first answers were provided about 1840
by writers such as Domingo Sarmiento of Argentina and José
Victorino Lastarria of Chile, whom Zea describes as "pre-
positivists" because, before they became acquainted with the
works of Auguste Comte, they arrived independently at much
the same conclusions as the French writer and in much the
same way. That is, they fused in like manner the ideas of
the same predecessors, such as the eclectics with their sense
of history, Saint-Simon with his social preoccupations, and
the utilitarians and the Scottish school with their predilection
for the experimental and the positive.

Consequently, when the works of Auguste Comte himself
became generally known in Latin America, as they did in the
third quarter of the nineteenth century, the ground had al-

[1] Leopoldo Zea, *Dos etapas del pensamiento en Hispanoamérica* (Mexico
City, 1949), p. 43. Cited hereafter as *Dos etapas*. I have drawn heavily on
this excellent book throughout the relevant part of the present chapter, and
also upon the illuminating account in chs. ii and iii of W. Rex Crawford, *A
Century of Latin American Thought* (Cambridge, 1944).

ready been so well prepared that his ideas gained immediate acceptance. Comtian positivism soon developed into a veritable cult all the way from Mexico to Argentina, and in Brazil as well as in Spanish America. This cult dominated Latin American thought in the last quarter of the nineteenth century, and its general outlook was strengthened rather than weakened by its only serious rival, the evolutionism of Darwin and his interpreters, Spencer and Huxley.

Those aspects of Latin American positivism which are especially significant for our purpose are, first, its liberalism, and second, its Americanism, which contained a strong ingredient of anti-Europeanism. Except in Mexico, where it was converted into an instrument of the dictatorship of Porfirio Díaz, positivism was generally identified with political liberalism. And even in Mexico it tempered the dictatorship by strengthening the rule of law, and, in Hegelian terminology, extended liberty from the one, if not to the many at any rate to the few. In all countries, including Mexico, it was dedicated to the promotion of education and material betterment for all classes of society. Writes Zea:

Thus, between 1880 and 1900 a new Hispanic America seemed to be emerging. . . . A new order arose in each country, not the rejected theological and colonial order, but one based upon science and concerned with educating its citizens and promoting their material welfare. . . . It was an era of progress and therefore of great optimism. In politics, its watchwords were liberty, progress, and democracy based upon scientific, positive foundations.[2]

Though positivism was European in origin, its popularity with the Latin Americans was a proof of their profound and growing Americanism, for it was popular precisely because it provided them with the means of developing and expressing their own American culture. The Chilean Lastarria said,

[2] Zea, *Dos etapas,* pp. 52–53.

"We must use European science and get all we can from it, but we must adapt it to our own needs and must never forget that we are first and foremost Americans, that is to say, democrats"; and the Argentine Juan Bautista Alberdi went him one better by advocating the development of an "American philosophy." [3]

Alberdi did in fact discuss America's role in world affairs in a way which might be called philosophical in the eighteenth-century usage of the term. His conclusions are of special interest for us because he anticipated some of the most effective twentieth-century criticisms of the Western Hemisphere idea and yet ended up by strongly endorsing its political application. His most mature thought on the subject is set forth in his book *El crimen de la guerra* (*The Crime of War*), written in 1870, and particularly in the chapter entitled "Pueblo-Mundo," which can be freely translated as "One World." Developing the theme of this title, Alberdi wrote:

In proportion as space is annihilated by the marvelous power of steam and electricity, . . . the nations of the world find themselves brought closer and closer together, so that they seem to form a single country. . . . Every railway is worth a dozen alliances; every foreign loan is a frontier wiped out. The three Atlantic cables [recently laid] have destroyed and buried the Monroe Doctrine without the least formality. . . . "Divided by the sea," the ancients said, because they were not seafaring peoples. "United by the sea" is the modern expression, for to seafaring peoples like the moderns, the sea is a bridge which unites the shores around it.[4]

Yet as Alberdi's argument proceeds, we learn that in his view the annihilation of space is still so far from complete that the peoples of the world have yet to pass through a stage of

[3] Zea, *América como conciencia,* pp. 126–127.
[4] Translation of passages quoted in Silva, *op. cit.,* pp. 32–36.

regional or continental organization before they will be ready for the final stage, the global. Examples given of the intermediate stage are "the United States of Europe" and "the union of the American world"—"continental sections," he calls them. And he makes it clear that by "the American world" he means both Americas (*ambas Américas*).[5]

In much of this pro-American literature, there was an implicit antagonism toward Europe. In the late 1850's and 60's it became explicit when Count Gobineau published his *Essai sur l'inégalité des races humaines* (1853–1855) and Napoleon III invaded Mexico and set up the empire of Maximilian of Hapsburg there (1861–1867). Lastarria promptly published in 1856 a counterblast to Gobineau, entitled with massive simplicity *La América,* in which he ridiculed the whole racist doctrine and declared that it had been invented for the purpose of justifying the domination of the North European peoples over the allegedly "inferior" races of Latin America.

In the next decade Napoleon's Mexican venture seemed to prove Lastarria's point, and another Chilean writer, Francisco Bilbao, in a book entitled *La América en peligro* (*America in Danger*) carried the war to the enemy's country. Our fathers, he said, believed that all their ideas of freedom came from France; but they were badly mistaken, for "France has never been free. France has never practiced liberty. . . . We must root out the erroneous ideas [our fathers had] and free ourselves from our spiritual servility towards France." But France was not the only offender; England and all Europe were equally guilty. "Away, then," he concluded, "with what is called European civilization. Europe, which cannot civilize itself, would fain civilize us. Europe . . . is the antinomy of America." [6]

[5] *Ibid.*, p. 35. See also Crawford, *op. cit.*, pp. 30–37.
[6] Zea, *Dos etapas,* pp. 126–127.

Sarmiento

But what was America? More and more, the Latin American writers of the positivist decades tended, though sometimes reluctantly and always with reservations, to see in the United States the clearest expression of what they meant by Americanism. Sarmiento wrote in these terms even in the midst of the United States' war of 1846–1848 with Mexico. He was in the minority then, but this became the majority in the momentous decade of the 1860's, when the European menace materialized in France's invasion of Mexico and in Spain's reoccupation of Santo Domingo and aggression against Peru; when the United States gave steady moral support to the aggrieved Mexican government of Juárez; and when the United States' abolition of slavery deprived its Latin American critics of one of their strongest talking points, and the cessation of its filibustering and territorial expansion southward deprived them of most of the rest. By 1864 Bilbao, formerly one of the Union's bitterest critics, was writing that "alliance with the United States will give us the leadership of the civilized world." [7]

It was Sarmiento, however, who was the most notable exponent in his lifetime (which lasted from 1811 to 1888) of what, as the antonym of Yankeephobia, may be called Yankeephilia. To describe Sarmiento as only a Yankeephile, however, would be to underrate both the breadth of his vision, which extended beyond the Western Hemisphere, and his devotion to his own country, which was boundless.[8] He was that rare being, the cosmopolitan patriot.

His cosmopolitanism is not a little surprising when we recall that he was born and brought up in a remote interior

[7] *Ibid.*, p. 128. See also Nathan L. Ferris, "The Relations of the United States with South America during the Civil War," *Hispanic American Historical Review,* XXI (1941), 51–78.

[8] Rojas, *op. cit.*, p. 316.

province of Argentina, far back among the foothills of the Andes, and that in the years of his early manhood Argentina was under the iron rule of a dictator, Juan Manuel de Rosas, whose regime was characterized by a high degree of nationalism and xenophobia. An interesting parallel is afforded by the case of his North American opposite number and junior by some twenty years, James G. Blaine, who was born in a little mountain town at the western extremity of Pennsylvania and grew up in the period when isolationism was at its zenith in the United States. But new winds of doctrine were astir in the Americas, and both men responded to them.

From our point of view, Sarmiento's basic ideas may be considered under two aspects, negative and positive; both reflected the influence of the eighteenth-century Enlightenment. Negatively, he sought to eradicate the Spanish tradition, for at this stage he was a firm believer in the *leyenda negra*, the "black legend" about Spain, which he regarded as the embodiment of all that was worst in the Europe of the Old Regime—clerical, feudal, bigoted, backward. His private war with the Argentine tyrant Rosas confirmed and strengthened him in this view, for Rosas represented, among other things, a reaction in favor of the Spanish creole tradition and against the liberal, cosmopolitan policies of the leading Argentine statesman of the early 1820's, Bernardino Rivadavia, who anticipated many of Sarmiento's ideas. Positively, Sarmiento looked to France for guidance and inspiration—the France of liberty, equality, and fraternity, of science and progress.

In 1845, however, just after the publication of his masterpiece, *Facundo,* he began a two-year trip to Europe and the United States which destroyed his faith in France and gave him a new shrine at which to worship—the United States.[9] On his trip to Europe he visited several countries, but in view

[9] Bunkley, *op. cit.,* pp. 245–298.

of the previous orientation of his thought, it is not surprising that his attention was focused mainly upon Spain and France. In Spain he found full confirmation of his preconceived notions. Viewed at first hand, Spain seemed just as bad as he had pictured it from across the Atlantic. The one constructive idea he acquired during his visit there—it was one he borrowed from the reforming Spanish writer Mariano José de Larra—was that the only hope of saving Spain lay in "Europeanizing" it; that is, in making it over in accordance with those ideas of liberty, science, and progress, which, for Sarmiento, had hitherto found their best expression in France.

As for France itself, however, Sarmiento's grand tour resulted not in confirmation of his earlier notions but in disillusionment. At the time of his visit, the Orleanist monarchy was tottering toward its fall, and Sarmiento was deeply shocked by the picture which French society presented to him: political corruption and social injustice, the selfishness, complacency, and stagnation of the ruling classes, and the brutish debasement of the masses. If France was the best Europe had to offer (and he still thought it was, in spite of everything), then Europeanization might help Spain, where conditions were so bad that no change could fail to bring an improvement, but no good Spanish American could want it applied to his part of the world. A little later his disillusionment was completed by the failure of the liberal revolutions of 1848 in Europe, and particularly by the aftermath of the one in France.

Bereft of his French model, Sarmiento recrossed the Atlantic in 1847; but he was seeking a new model to replace it, and this he found in the United States that same year. His enthusiasm for the latter never wavered to the end of his life forty-one years later and was only increased by a second and longer visit, as Argentine minister to the United States from 1865 to 1868.

It was in the course of this second visit that Sarmiento's enthusiasm for the United States carried him to the point of publicly endorsing the Monroe Doctrine. His endorsement of it was truly a historic event. It had no precedent in the annals of Argentine foreign policy; a generation later it served as the first of the only two precedents cited by the Foreign Minister of Argentina, Luis M. Drago, in reply to Argentine criticism of his "economic corollary to the Monroe Doctrine," [10] which will be discussed in the next chapter. Sarmiento's endorsement was given only upon condition that the Monroe Doctrine be properly interpreted; that is to say, that it be interpreted as a doctrine of equality and reciprocity among the nations of the Western Hemisphere, not a doctrine of the United States' hegemony or imperialism.

Originally skeptical about inter-American co-operation, Sarmiento had by this time become a convert to it—witness his participation in the Lima Congress of 1864–1865, to which reference has already been made. He believed that such co-operation would be more useful in the cultural than in the political field; but "cultural" must be understood here in a broad sense, for while his conception of the hemispheric interchange gave first place to such things as education, books, and ideas, it also gave a very prominent place to such other things as technology and business enterprise. He freely admitted that, for a good many years to come, the chief benefits of the interchange would be conferred by the United States and received by the Latin American nations. Thus, in his principal public statement on the subject, an address to the Rhode Island Historical Society in 1865, he devoted most of his time to relating how a host of Yankee entrepreneurs and technicians had contributed to the economic development, and, through this, to the social and political betterment, of many

[10] Silva, *op. cit.*, pp. 498–499, note dated May 9, 1906.

70

parts of Latin America. This, he concluded, is the right kind of Monroe Doctrine in action.[11]

Despite certain inconsistencies and deviations—he was not a systematic thinker—we may regard the foregoing as representative of Sarmiento's mature thought on the subject of hemispheric relations. His reasoning was based upon an interpretation of history and upon the conclusions drawn from his trip to Europe and the United States from 1845 to 1847 and reinforced by later experience. It seems to have run thus: Several decades of bitter experience had proved that Spanish American society as then constituted was incapable of achieving stability, order, and progress, either within the borders of the separate states or in their relations with one another. Radical reform and modernization were necessary, and they must come from abroad. They could not be provided by Europe; nothing that had happened since his disillusionment with France in 1846 had altered his opinion on this point. Rather, much of what had happened had strengthened it and made him feel not only that, as Bilbao put it, Europe was incapable of civilizing itself but that the Old World was in truth senescent and therefore no fit model for the youthful nations of the New World.

The United States, on the other hand, was for him the model of what a New World nation should be and one that the rest of them could and must follow. Accordingly, the Latin American nations must "North Americanize" themselves and draw closer to the United States in a hemispheric association conceived in the spirit of the Monroe Doctrine, properly interpreted. They would thereby achieve the desired order, progress, and liberty, and ultimately they would give as well as receive benefits. Thus, in his last message to Congress as

[11] Allison W. Bunkley, ed., *A Sarmiento Anthology* (Princeton, 1948), pp. 315–332.

President of Argentina, Sarmiento said in 1874 that even as the United States had originated the great principle of religious toleration, so South America ought to originate, through inter-American channels, the principle of the suppression of war, on the model of the bilateral arbitration treaty between Argentina and the United States which he had proposed while minister at Washington.[12]

Sarmiento's ideas may seem somewhat impractical, but they were conceived in a practical spirit. The most rigorous analysis would detect in them hardly a trace of the Western Hemisphere mysticism of, for example, Jefferson's letter of 1813 to Alexander von Humboldt. Rather, they were a product of the positivist attitude which, as we have seen, had been taken by Sarmiento even before the positivist philosophy was naturalized in Latin America. In the last decade or so of his life, positivism was at the height of its vogue there; and this goes far to explain why Sarmiento in his later years may be taken as representing a large body of Latin American opinion not only in his general approach to public problems but also in many of his specific opinions about them, such as those regarding Europe and the United States in their relation to Latin America.

Thus, one element in the intellectual climate of the Atlantic world at that time was the belief that the European system of monarchy was decadent and that the republican system, with the United States as its chief exponent, represented the "wave of the future." This belief was expressed in James Bryce's book *The American Commonwealth,* published in 1888,[13] and it contributed to the Brazilian revolution of

[12] Silva, *op. cit.,* p. 30.

[13] Bryce wrote that the institutions of the United States were "something more than an experiment, for they are believed to disclose and display the type of institutions towards which, as by a law of fate, the rest of civilized mankind are forced to move, some with swifter, others with slower, but all with unresting feet."

1889–1891, which overthrew the imperial government of that country and replaced it with a republican government modeled closely upon that of the United States.

Generally speaking, moreover, the relations of the United States with the Latin American countries now took a turn for the better, conspicuously so in the case of its next-door neighbor, Mexico. The chief exception was Chile, with which there were serious incidents and strained relations for more than a decade after 1880; but this cost the United States little or nothing in the good will of the rest of Latin America, since at this time Chile herself was only too successfully playing the game of manifest destiny and territorial expansion at the expense of her neighbors, Bolivia and Peru. Though the United States still clung to its hard and fast isolationism at the beginning of this period, there were soon signs that this was weakening where Latin America was concerned.

Many Latin Americans were now in a receptive mood, all the more so because in this same period European capital and business enterprise began to penetrate Latin America on a large scale. Great Britain led the march, and its deepest penetration was made in Argentina, which by 1890 was being described, only half-jokingly, as a British colony. France and Germany came next, followed by almost every other European country; not a single country in Latin America was left untouched.

This process pleased not a few Latin Americans, because not a few of them profited by it, but it also alarmed others as a new and insidious form of imperialism. It promised benefits but threatened domination; the European investors and entrepreneurs, according to this view, were Achaeans bringing gifts. Economics aside, there was a political danger, which was twofold. In its crude form, this lay in the fact that the European powers were making more and more use of armed intervention to protect their expanding economic interests

73

all over the world; Napoleon III's five-year intrusion into Mexico was a glaring example of the application of this measure to Latin America.[14] In its subtler form, economic penetration could lead to political penetration. About 1860 Argentina's neighbors thought they saw an example of this in the refusal of its government to support the movement for Spanish American union, for they attributed the refusal to pressure from European business interests in Buenos Aires.

This situation, too, favored the United States. The latter had never practiced intervention; it helped to force the termination of the French intervention in Mexico in 1866; and before 1890 its investments in Latin America were microscopic, except in Mexico, where they were exceeded by those of Great Britain.

Blaine and other Pan Americanists

In these propitious circumstances, the United States launched the modern Pan American movement in the 1880's and brought the term "Pan American" into use. First employed in 1882, by a New York newspaper,[15] the term gained common currency during the inter-American conference at Washington in 1889–1890. Here again we see the influence of Europe, for Pan American was obviously derived from the earlier Pan-Slav and Pan-German movements.

Among the many reasons why the Pan American movement got under way at this time, three should be mentioned. First, Blaine and others were alarmed lest continued international conflict in Latin America should lead to European interven-

[14] J. Fred Rippy, *Latin America in World Politics* (3d ed., New York, 1938), pp. 126–127, and Robert N. Frazer, "Latin American Projects to Aid Mexico During the French Intervention," *Hispanic American Historical Review*, XXVIII (1948), 377–388. For a general account of this European development, see Carleton J. H. Hayes, *A Generation of Materialism, 1871–1900* (New York, 1941).

[15] New York *Evening Post,* June 27, 1882 (Lockey, *op. cit.,* p. 2).

tion.[16] One such conflict, involving Argentina, Brazil, Uruguay, and Paraguay, had lasted from 1865 to 1870. Another, involving Chile, Peru, and Bolivia, broke out in 1879. In Blaine's opinion this situation called urgently for the establishment of inter-American peace machinery. In the second place, in 1879–1880 the famous French engineer Ferdinand de Lesseps organized a company to build an interoceanic canal at Panama. The company was organized under French law and had its headquarters in Paris, but it was to operate under a concession from a Latin American government, Colombia. The enterprise was one which possessed great strategic as well as commercial importance for the United States and one which it had had in mind for itself ever since the time of Henry Clay. Here, then, was a striking proof of the way in which European private enterprise as well as government action could effect a penetration of Latin America to the direct injury of the United States. Obviously, it was time for the latter to bestir itself with its southern neighbors. In the third place, the economic situation in the United States taught the same lesson. Since the Civil War there had been a great increase in the production of the country's factories, farms, and silver mines. By the 1880's all three branches of the nation's economy were looking for foreign outlets; if these could be found in Latin America, they would serve an economic as well as a political purpose.

As is well known, the first Pan American launching, which took place in 1881, proved abortive. In March of that year Blaine was appointed Secretary of State by President James A. Garfield, and in November he issued invitations to the other American governments for an international conference on "the means of preventing war among the nations of Amer-

---

[16] Alice Felt Tyler, *The Foreign Policy of James G. Blaine* (Minneapolis, 1927), pp. 165–190; A. Curtis Wilgus, "Blaine and Pan Americanism," *Hispanic American Historical Review,* V (1922), 662–708.

ica." In the meantime, however, Garfield was assassinated. His successor, Chester A. Arthur, first approved the issuance of the invitations, but the following month (December) he replaced Blaine with a new Secretary of State, Frederick T. Frelinghuysen, who after a short delay recalled the invitations mainly on the ground that the War of the Pacific, in progress since 1879 between Chile and allied Bolivia and Peru, had not been terminated as expected.

The cancellation of the conference provoked no general protest in the United States. Clearly, Blaine's move had been premature. If the project was to be carried out, a broader base of public support must be built up.

The process by which this was accomplished in less than a decade possesses a special interest for students of the history of the Western Hemisphere idea. The three major points of interest are, first, that although Blaine was the most important figure in the Pan American movement, it was the product of many other hands as well; second, that the hemispheric idea was accepted even by critics of the particular form in which it was expressed in this movement; and third, that now, as earlier, the form of expression of the idea was determined partly by antipathy towards Europe but partly also by imitation of Europe.

Blaine's title to leadership in the movement is clear. In his short term in 1881 he did a great deal to revive the Hemisphere idea in the United States. Without sacrificing the idea, he extended the American system to include Hawaii, which he described as the Cuba of the Pacific. While his Americanism was strongly nationalistic, it was curiously blended with continentalism. He repeated Secretary Everett's claim of 1852 that the United States had a paramount interest in Cuba and he challenged Great Britain with a similar claim regarding Panama, and yet at the same time he widened from Caribbean to hemispheric scope Everett's vision of "the ceaseless movement of segregation of American interests from European control and [their] unification in a broader American sphere of independent life." [17] By "America" Everett usually meant the United States; by "America" Blaine frequently meant the whole hemisphere.

On the other hand, from Blaine's resignation as Secretary of State in December 1881 until his return to that post in 1889, he was mainly occupied with other matters than Pan Americanism, such as his unsuccessful campaign for the presidency of the United States in 1884. In this seven-year interval the task of promoting the Pan American movement devolved upon others, including members of Congress such as William McKinley of Ohio, future President of the United States, and John T. Morgan of Alabama, who was soon to lead the fight for the Nicaragua canal route, and publicists such as Hinton Rowan Helper and William Eleroy Curtis. Their efforts were conspicuously successful, and it was they, not Blaine, who were responsible for the calling of the Pan American conference at which he presided in 1889. Moreover, in the meantime they had added to the single objective of his conference plans of 1881 (the prevention of war) several more, among which were the establishment of an "American Customs Union" and better steamship communications, the construction of a Pan American railway, and the adoption of uniform customs regulations, trade-mark and copyright laws, and a common silver coin.[18] All agreed that the question of politico-military alliances was not to be included; this was not to be another Panama Congress.

[17] Ruhl J. Bartlett, ed., *The Record of American Diplomacy* (New York, 1947), p. 359.

[18] This broadening of the agenda is illustrated by the documents on this subject conveniently brought together in International American Conference, *Reports of Committees*, vol. IV, *Historical Appendix: The Congress of 1826 at Panama and Subsequent Movements towards a Conference of American Nations* (Washington, 1890), pp. 255–258, 310–375. This volume will hereafter be referred to as *Historical Appendix*.

The two publicists mentioned above played an important part in this propagandizing process. Hinton Rowan Helper, self-styled "the new Christopher Columbus," is best known to students of the domestic history of the United States as the author of a tract, *The Impending Crisis,* published on the eve of the Civil War, which made a great noise in the growing controversy between North and South. To students of the diplomatic history of the United States and inter-American relations, he ought to be better known than he is as a pioneer of the Pan American movement, for he was one of its most energetic and effective promoters, rivaling Blaine himself in this respect. As a political reward for his book, *The Impending Crisis,* he was appointed in 1861 American consul in Buenos Aires, a post which he held for the next five years. This gave him an interest in the promotion of commerce between the United States and South America which lasted the rest of his life. After his return to his own country, he devoted himself to the subject with missionary zeal, memorializing congress, writing two books and thousands of letters, and interviewing hundreds of influential men.[19]

At that time the United States had only recently strengthened the bonds of its own national union by completing its first transcontinental railways from the Atlantic to the Pacific. Not unnaturally, then, Helper chose for the core of his plan of hemispheric union the construction of a Pan American railway from the United States to southern South America.[20] This was unfortunate for him, since it identified him with a project which, as it turned out, was never seriously attempted, though interminably discussed. In 1880, however, he coupled

[19] "Hinton Rowan Helper," *Dictionary of American Biography,* VIII (New York, 1932), 517–518. For further details about Helper and the railway project, see John Anthony Caruso, "The Pan American Railway," *Hispanic American Historical Review,* XXXI (1951), 608–639.

[20] *Historical Appendix,* pp. 293–295.

it with the idea of an inter-American conference and got the first bill for this purpose introduced into Congress; [21] and this project ultimately bore fruit. Another bill which he inspired in 1882 led in 1884 to the sending of a commercial mission to tour Latin America,[22] and this in turn led to the meeting of the first Pan American Conference in 1889. Helper himself got no reward. Pushed aside and forgotten, he died twenty years later in poverty and by his own hand.

More fortunate was the other of these two Pan American publicists, William Eleroy Curtis. Born and educated in Ohio, Curtis spent a decade in newspaper work in Chicago [23] before he first became prominently identified with international affairs through his appointment in 1884 as secretary (later, member) of the commercial mission to Latin America. He returned from this mission an ardent Pan Americanist and one of its best propagandists. He seems to have been the chief author of the mission's voluminous and enthusiastic reports, which were published by the United States Congress as official documents; and he followed these up with eloquent and effective testimony before the appropriate committees of Congress,[24] with articles which he wrote as Washington correspondent of a Chicago newspaper, and with a book, *The Capitals of Spanish America* (1888), which, though offensive to some Latin Americans, was well received in the United States. Unlike Helper, he had his reward. When in 1890 the first Pan American Conference created the Commercial Bureau of the American Republics (later developed into the Pan American Union), he was made its first director.

In support of the proposition that even critics of the Pan

[21] *Ibid.*, p. 293. Senator David Davis of Illinois introduced this bill, "by request of Mr. Hinton Rowan Helper," on January 21, 1880.

[22] *Ibid.*, pp. 294, 298, 308–309.

[23] "William Eleroy Curtis," *Dictionary of American Biography,* IV (New York, 1930), 620–621.

[24] See, for example, his address before the Senate Committee on Foreign Relations, *Historical Appendix,* pp. 360–373.

American movement accepted the Hemisphere idea, only two instances need be cited. One was provided by Secretary of State Frelinghuysen. Though he had recalled Blaine's conference invitations of 1881, he made it clear that while he was opposed to such a conference as the initial step in achieving the Pan American objective, he was not opposed to the objective itself. Quite the contrary; he told Congress in 1884:

I am thoroughly convinced of the desirability of knitting closely our relations with the States of this continent . . . in the spirit of the Monroe Doctrine, which, in excluding foreign political interference, recognizes the common interest of the States of North and South America.[25]

The other instance comes from the minority report presented in 1886 by Congressman Perry Belmont of New York in opposition to the calling of a Pan American conference. Far from dissenting from the hemispheric faith, he spoke only with sympathy of "this Western Hemisphere," "this continent," and "the neighboring governments on this continent"; one of his chief objections to the proposed conference was that it would not be truly hemispheric since it would not include either Canada or the European possessions in the West Indies.[26]

The familiar pattern of antipathy towards Europe combined with imitation of Europe reappeared at this time. The antipathy was motivated primarily by the rapid progress of European economic penetration of Latin America. Thus, in 1884, the sponsor of one of the Pan American bills in Congress quoted Helper as saying:

[On my travels through South America] it always grieved me exceedingly, and was particularly offensive to my sense of the fitness of things, to find [that] almost everything in the way of foreign

[25] *Ibid.*, p. 300.   [26] *Ibid.*, pp. 320–329.

merchandise . . . [was] of European manufacture. . . . From the little pin with which the lady fastens her beau-catching ribbons to the grand piano with which she enlivens and enchants the hearts of all her household; from the tiniest thread and tack and tool . . . to the largest plows and harrows . . . [all] are, with rare exceptions, of English, German, Spanish, or Italian make.

The congressman then continued on his own account that, if his Pan-American project were carried out, the United States would be "in a position to say to Europe in the memorable words of President Monroe: 'that we should consider any attempt on their part to extend their system to any portion of this hemisphere as dangerous to our peace and safety.' " [27]

William Eleroy Curtis made the same point in his testimony before a committee of Congress in 1886, but he painted the picture of European penetration in even darker colors, pointing out that the position of the United States in South America had greatly deteriorated in the past twenty years and would continue to do so unless the government promptly took remedial measures. "The cause of this astonishing phenomenon," he explained, "is our neglect to furnish the ways and means of commerce," and this neglect is due to our "even more astonishing" ignorance of the "condition and progress" of South America. "Chili, Uruguay, Paraguay, and the Argentine Republic . . . are booming like our Western Territories," he said, but they are "almost *terra incognita* to us," and so the benefits of the boom have gone exclusively to "the three commercial nations of Europe"—England, France, and Germany. Moreover, he warned, these three nations "have secured a monopoly of the trade of Spanish America [at large, and] . . . the Englishmen have the Brazilians by the throat." [28]

[27] *Ibid.*, pp. 305, 307.   [28] *Ibid.*, pp. 360, 363.

81

American Zollverein

Yet in defending America against Europe, there was just as much readiness to profit by the example of Europe as there had been sixty years earlier when Henry Clay advocated the union of the Americas as an imitative counterpoise to the Holy Alliance. In the present case, the example was provided by Germany: the success of the *Zollverein* in promoting the unification of the separate German states was avowedly the inspiration of the project for an "American Customs Union," which was one of the main items on the agenda of the first Pan American Conference. The influence of Germany's example was made crystal clear by the chief sponsor of the project, Thomas C. Reynolds, of St. Louis, Missouri. Reynolds had been a member of the recent commercial mission to Latin America; he had also previously spent several years in Germany. Writing in 1886 in support of a Senate bill intended "to promote the political progress and commercial prosperity of the American nations" by calling an inter-American conference to consider a customs union and other measures, Reynolds observed that such a conference offered "peculiar advantages" to "our hemisphere" and that the history of the *Zollverein* was particularly instructive for this purpose. Composed at first only of Prussia and a few minor contiguous states and resisted for one reason or another by the rest, the *Zollverein*, he said, had required sixty years to bring

the union [of German states] up to its present extent and importance. . . . Here, as in Germany . . . like obstacles will be removed by like means. Should even but one [American] State be willing to unite with us [at the outset] . . . the adhesion of all the others to a complete commercial and customs union [of the American nations] will be a question of time—probably of half a century.[29]

[29] *Ibid.*, pp. 347–348, 349.

Throughout the discussions of these years, there was a conscious reassertion of the hemispheric idea which lay at the base of the Monroe Doctrine, a reassertion which made explicit its clear implication that the nations of the Western Hemisphere stood in a special relationship to one another. Thus, S. O. Thacher, another member of the recent commercial mission to Latin America, said in 1886 that the combination of geographical propinquity and historic fact "imposes upon us a different relation to those [Latin American] peoples than that which we hold to other nations." [30] In two respects, however, the Pan Americanists of this decade carried the Hemisphere idea beyond the point to which Monroe in 1823, or even Adams and Clay in 1826, had carried it. Unlike Monroe, they proposed to implement the "special relationship" through positive inter-American co-operation; and unlike Adams and Clay, they conceived of this co-operation primarily in economic, not political terms, but they did so (it is important to note) on the assumption that, once economic solidarity had been achieved, political solidarity would follow as a matter of course.

These differences are explained by the changed circumstances of the 1880's, especially by the rapidly advancing economic conquest of Latin America by Europe. The *Zollverein* seemed to offer the best type of defense against this threat, for it was a form of international co-operation that had proved both its economic utility and its efficacy for political unification. Hence the heavy stress which the Pan Americanists laid on the project for a commercial and customs union of the Americas. This project was given first place in the Act of Congress of 1888 which led to the Pan American Conference of 1889–1890 in Washington.

So successfully had the Pan Americanists done their work of persuasion that, in the face of opposition from President

[30] *Ibid.,* p. 338.

Cleveland and his Secretary of State, bipartisan majorities in the two houses of Congress passed (in May 1888) an act directing the President to issue invitations for an inter-American conference. That the Hemisphere idea was still fluid is shown by the guest list. Canada was included in it in the original bill but not in the final act. The Kingdom of Hawaii, to which Blaine had extended the Monroe Doctrine, was included but did not accept in time. The Latin American states completed the list; among them was the Empire of Brazil.

President Cleveland let the act become law without his signature.[31] The invitations were issued under his Democratic administration, but by the time the Pan American Conference met at Washington, in 1889, the Republicans were back in power, and Blaine, again Secretary of State, was its presiding officer. In short, when it was at last successfully launched, the Pan American movement in the United States was not identified exclusively with either party but represented a national policy which had solid support in the nation at large.

So far as the customs union project was concerned, the conference was a complete and disillusioning failure. As the meeting drew slowly toward its close, this project was killed by an overwhelmingly adverse vote, and the Argentine delegate Roque Sáenz Peña drove a nail in its coffin with an eloquent and long-remembered speech in which he argued for universalism as against regionalism and said: "What I lack is not love for America, but suspicion and ingratitude towards Europe. I cannot forget that in Europe are Spain, our mother; Italy, our friend; and France, our elder sister." And alluding to the catch phrase of the customs-unionists, "America for the Americans," he offered in its stead the motto, "America for all mankind." [32]

[31] *Ibid.*, p. 375.   [32] Silva, *op. cit.*, p. 45.

Otherwise, the conference was successful in comparison with its inter-American predecessors. It was far better attended than any of them: all but one of the Latin American states (the Dominican Republic) took part in it. Also, unlike its predecessors, it took actions which lived after it, notably by adopting an arbitration convention which paved the way for the elaborate inter-American peace system of the present day and by establishing a permanent organ, the Commercial Bureau of the American Republics, which, as already noted, subsequently grew into the Pan American Union. Though the sum total of its achievements was far from impressive, it was promising. Yet the conference did nothing about the problem of European economic penetration to which the rejected customs union project was addressed and which was to develop in a still more aggravated form in the next dozen years.

V

Drago's Economic Corollary

to the Monroe Doctrine

EARLY in December 1902, naval forces of Germany and Great Britain started an armed intervention against Venezuela in an effort to collect debts due their subjects. Italy soon joined in the intervention. Venezuela resisted, and the fighting that followed resulted in the loss of Venezuelan lives as well as property.

The true Drago Doctrine

Excitement and indignation flared up all over America. Argentina, which Britain had just been pressing for the payment of overdue debts, was no exception.[1] Accordingly, be-

[1] According to Drago, speaking in 1914, the intervention of 1902 in Venezuela provoked in Buenos Aires an agitation which "llegó . . . a un estado de histerismo" (Silva, *op. cit.*, p. 506). Though apparently without any threat

fore the month was out, the Argentine Foreign Minister, Luis María Drago, dispatched a note to Washington (dated December 29, 1902) [2] which was intended to put a stop to this sort of thing by prohibiting the use of armed force by any European power against any American nation for the collection of a public debt. Though Drago himself did not attach the label to his proposal, it soon became known as the Drago Doctrine; and in 1907 a new version of it, proposed by the United States, was adopted by the Second Hague Peace Conference.

The latter fact explains why, in most of the extensive literature that has grown up about it, the Drago Doctrine is considered as a contribution to international law and is represented as having had the support of the United States.[3] If that were the whole truth, this essay would never have been written, since the matter would be of little concern to the historian of the Western Hemisphere idea. But it is true only of the end product at the Hague Conference of 1907, and that was so completely bowdlerized a version of the genuine Drago Doctrine that Drago himself opposed its adoption.

On the other hand, we are very much concerned with the genuine Drago Doctrine as proposed by the author in his note of December 29, 1902, and subsequently explained and

of intervention, the British government in 1902 made the large amount of overdue Argentine and Chilean debts to British subjects a ground for urging the governments of the two countries to avoid an arms race. Its pressure may have contributed to their conclusion of the *Pactos de Mayo* of that year, which included an agreement limiting naval armaments.

[2] The original Spanish text and the State Department's English translation, as published in *Papers Relating to the Foreign Relations of the United States,* are conveniently brought together in Mariano J. Drago, *Luis Drago, discursos y escritos* (Buenos Aires, 1938), II, 49–56, 59–66. See also note 15, below. For a good brief summary of the Drago Doctrine and its history from the point of view of international law, with references, see E. M. Borchard, "Calvo and Drago Doctrines," *Encyclopaedia of the Social Sciences,* III (New York, 1930), 153–156.

[3] Bemis, *Latin American Policy,* p. 147.

defended by him, for this was a highly important contribution to the history of the Western Hemisphere idea. Drago designed his proposal not for the whole world but only for the Western Hemisphere, and not as an amendment to international law but as policy; he likened it in this respect to the Monroe Doctrine and described it as an economic corollary to the latter.[4] There was, however, an important difference between the two, for Monroe's doctrine was a unilateral national policy of the United States, whereas Drago's was intended to become a multilateral inter-American policy. He even tried to get Brazil and Chile to join with him in proposing it in the first place, and though their reluctance and the urgency of the situation forced him to act alone, the very terms of the proposal contemplated their ultimate participation, along with that of the other American states, in supporting his Western Hemisphere doctrine.

Finally, Drago's proposal was a new departure in Argentine foreign policy, and if the United States had accepted it, perhaps the whole future history of United States–Argentine relations and of inter-American relations in general might have been changed for the better. Instead, the United States opposed the true Drago Doctrine, and by 1906 the Argentine government had reverted to its traditional policy of coolness towards both the Monroe Doctrine and American regionalism. The United States' opposition to the Drago Doctrine was never open, but it was clear and effective—that is the meaning of its successful effort to get the denatured Drago Doctrine adopted by the Hague Conference. Moreover, in the meanwhile the United States had come forth with its own alternative prescription for the problem of European intervention to which Drago's proposal was addressed. This, too, was a corollary to the Monroe Doctrine—the Roosevelt corollary

[4] See below, note 17.

of 1904–1905; but unlike Drago's, it was strictly unilateral.

Thus, there was a clash between two diametrically opposite interpretations of the Western Hemisphere idea: Drago's interpretation, which was multilateral, and the United States government's, which was unilateral. This conflict for control of the Western Hemisphere idea forms the central theme of this essay.

Two caveats should be entered at this point. In the first place, Drago's doctrine will be considered in the sense in which he proposed it, that is, not as international law but as policy. He disclaimed any special proficiency in international law and rather proved his point by erroneously identifying the issue in Venezuela as one of public debt, whereas it was in fact very largely one of private claims. In the second place, many of the details of this episode remain conjectural, for the Argentine official sources still remain closed to scholars, and while the United States sources have long been open, they are silent on several important points. Nevertheless, it is believed that the major outlines of the story that follows rest on a firm foundation, and that only details, mainly in the matter of motivation, remain to be filled in.

In order to understand how the conflict for control of the Western Hemisphere idea arose and was settled, we must first turn back for a brief survey of certain developments that had occurred in America since the first Pan American Conference, held at Washington in 1889–1890. These developments will be discussed mainly from the point of view of the United States, whose position prevailed in the conflict in question.

The impact of the capitalist-industrial system

Europe's expanding capitalist-industrial system had affected the economies of both Americas greatly but with widely different results. In the case of Latin America,[5] the result had been to intensify the colonial character of that area in the economic sense. It was becoming more and more a producer of foodstuffs and raw materials for the great industrial states and more and more a debtor to financial interests in those states, whose growing investments were giving them an ever-tighter hold over its means of production and distribution.

The United States, on the other hand, had taken a leaf out of Europe's book by duplicating the latter's development of a great capitalist-industrial system. At some points, indeed, the United States had even gone Europe one better; thus, the United States Steel Corporation, founded in 1901, was the largest aggregation of steel mills in the world. Though still a debtor nation on balance, the United States was obviously moving towards a creditor position; it had already built up investments on a large scale in Mexico and on a considerable scale in Cuba and Canada and was looking abroad for new fields for investment as well as for wider markets. In short, by 1900 the mature, expanding economy of the United States had given it an international position and outlook which was becoming more and more like that of the great powers of Western Europe and less and less like that of the economically backward debtor nations of Latin America.[6]

[5] There is an urgent need for a comprehensive and thorough study of this subject. Most of what has been written about it either relates to individual countries, e.g., J. Fred Rippy, "Argentina," ch. x, "The Economic Revolution and Educational Progress," in A. C. Wilgus, ed., *Argentina, Brazil, and Chile since Independence* (Washington, D.C., 1935), or is scattered through general accounts of Latin American economic development focused on the more recent period, such as those by Simon G. Hansen and Wendell C. Gordon. J. Fred Rippy, *Latin America and the Industrial Age* (2d ed., New York, 1947) deals mainly with transportation and communications. George Wythe, *Industry in Latin America* (New York, 1945), contains useful information, some of it historical, on various aspects of our problem, but it is primarily a study of industry in the contemporary period.

[6] Archibald Cary Coolidge, *The United States as a World Power* (New York, 1908), p. 177, linked one aspect of this change to the coolness of the

By the 1890's many people in the United States had a full sense of their country's great and growing strength and of the potentially revolutionary significance of this growth for their foreign policy. The realization was reflected in the increasing frequency with which they used the phrase "the rise of the United States to world power." Stressing its obligations as well as its rights in this new role, many of them clamored for more active participation by their country in international affairs.

Their clamor and the new direction which United States foreign policy took in this crucial decade were powerfully influenced by the new wave of European imperialism which swept over a large part of Asia and most of Africa in the second half of the nineteenth century.[7] At times the new imperialism was as open and direct as the older one, but it also operated in the new and subtler ways of economic penetration and spheres of influence, and that made it more dangerous. The danger increased as the century drew towards its close: new great powers (notably Germany) joined in the scramble for empire, the partition of Africa was completed, and that of China, chaotic and honeycombed with foreign concessions, seemed imminent. Would Latin America be next?

In the United States, the reaction to this new surge of

United States toward the Drago Doctrine, saying that "a generation or two ago the United States [as a debtor state] might have supported the Drago doctrine with enthusiasm . . . now it has supported at the Hague a much softened version, and it has aided San Domingo to satisfy her creditors, not to defy them." Further on, Coolidge broadened the analysis: "If, at the time of the promulgation of the Monroe Doctrine, it appeared to Americans that the New World differed from the Old chiefly in being the home of free governments in contrast to the lands ruled by the principle of authority, today . . . one of the main distinctions between Latin America and western Europe is that between debtor and creditor nations, but the interests of the Anglo-Saxon republic are no longer entirely on the side of the former" (*ibid.*, p. 297).

[7] The classic study of this subject is William L. Langer, *The Diplomacy of Imperialism, 1890–1902* (2 vols., New York, 1935).

European imperialism was partly defensive and partly imitative. The defensive reaction was expressed in Henry Cabot Lodge's warning in 1895, apropos of the boundary dispute between Venezuela and Great Britain, that the United States must not let South America become another Africa.[8] The imitative reaction was expressed not only in the overseas annexations of 1898 (Puerto Rico, Hawaii, and the Philippines) but also in the terms in which these annexations were rationalized, such as national honor and economic interest, racial superiority, the "white man's burden," and missionary zeal. The result was a new and seductive version of Manifest Destiny, which was given a hard core of strategy, based mainly on sea power, by Alfred Thayer Mahan, and was popularized by publicists such as Albert Shaw, founder (in 1890) and editor of the influential *American Monthly Review of Reviews*.[9]

Under the leadership of these men and influenced by the inexorable pressure of events, the monolithic isolationism of the previous three generations broke down in the 1890's. Whether this was in some measure due to the influence of British precept is uncertain, but it is at least an interesting coincidence that splendid isolation had begun to lose its splendor in Britain a decade earlier than in the United States.[10]

What supplanted isolationism in the United States was not a simple two-way schism between those who were for it and those who were against it, but a three-way split, for the anti-

[8] Dexter Perkins, *The Monroe Doctrine, 1867–1907* (Baltimore, 1937), pp. 150–151.

[9] Julius W. Pratt, *The Expansionists of 1898* (Baltimore, 1936), pp. 1–33, 188–229; Weinberg, *Manifest Destiny*, pp. 283 ff.

[10] Edward M. Earle, "A Half-Century of American Foreign Policy: Our Stake in Europe, 1898–1948," *Political Science Quarterly*, LXIV (1949), 170, holds that after 1898 the United States remained "perversely isolationist" only as regards the Old World, while it was interventionist in both the Far East and Latin America.

isolationists themselves were already tending to fall into the two groups that were to take definite shape in the twentieth century. In one group were the internationalists; in the other, the advocates of increased participation in world politics on a go-it-alone basis—in common parlance, the national imperialists. This threefold pattern has persisted to the present day, though since 1941 the lines have been blurred by the isolationists' taking to cover.

Between 1895 and 1902 successes won by the anti-isolationists, combined with events in other parts of the world, brought about an enduring revolution in the relations of the United States with two great powers, Russia and Britain. As applied in the Far East, Washington's more vigorous foreign policy led to friction with Russia and broke up the seventy-year-old "traditional friendship" between the two countries, which since then has never been securely mended. More important for this study was the great improvement that took place simultaneously in the relations of the United States with Great Britain. Hitherto, these had been characterized by frequently recurring tension. A great deal of this friction had had to do with Latin America; [11] from the time of George Canning on, it had to do with a certain lack of respect on the part of successive British governments for the Monroe Doctrine.[12] In 1896, in connection with the Venezuela boundary dispute, Britain reversed its attitude towards the Monroe Doctrine.[13] In the next few years it followed this up with other actions in the same spirit—notably its great concession in the Hay-Pauncefote Treaty of 1901 regarding the Panama Canal—the net effect of which was to give the United States a much freer hand in its relations with Latin America than it had ever had before. The result was the development of a

[11] An early phase is discussed in J. Fred Rippy, *Rivalry of the United States and Great Britain over Latin America (1808–1830)* (Baltimore, 1929).
[12] Bemis, *Latin American Policy,* pp. 107, 153.
[13] *Ibid.,* pp. 121–122.

kind of Anglo-American entente, the importance of which for our purpose can hardly be exaggerated.

In the freer atmosphere created by the nascent Anglo-American entente, the new forward policy of the United States won most of its major successes in the field of Western Hemisphere affairs, above all in the Caribbean area. Here it provided a striking illustration of that inner conflict between internationalism and imperialism in the United States to which reference has already been made. The trend towards imperialism proved to be decidedly the stronger of the two. Though the United States had so recently taken the initiative in launching the Pan American movement through the Washington Conference of 1889–1890 and had prodded its good friend Dictator Porfirio Díaz of Mexico into playing host to a second Pan American Conference in 1901–1902, the watchword at Washington was increasingly "go it alone." This is hardly surprising when we recall that by general agreement the politico-military objectives which had been pursued with so little success in the earlier inter-American conferences, from Panama in 1826 to Lima in 1865, were excluded from the purview of the new Pan American movement. Even the customs union project, which, though primarily economic, had strong political implications, was not revived after its failure at the first conference in 1890. Clearly, therefore, the Pan American movement was by definition not fitted to handle the type of Caribbean questions with which the "large" policy was concerned in this period.

Accordingly, the United States "went it alone" in handling these questions, even when they were obviously of great interest to some or all of the Latin American states. Before Foreign Minister Drago proposed his doctrine in 1902, the United States had acted unilaterally in several such cases—in that of the Venezuela boundary controversy with Britain of 1895–1896; in that of Cuba, which led to war with Spain in

1898; in the Isthmian Canal Treaty of 1901 with Great Britain; and in the very case of the Venezuelan debts which provoked Drago's note. Shortly thereafter it did so again in 1903 in the case of the secession of Panama from Colombia; and, as we shall see, it was soon to do so yet again in two cases that involved the whole Hemisphere—the Roosevelt corollary (1904) and Pan Americanism (1906). Finally, in his annual message at the beginning of December 1902, President Roosevelt had declared that the unilateral Monroe Doctrine was the cardinal principle of United States foreign policy.[14] In short, the government which carried out the large policy in America at this early period was one which had the habit of dealing unilaterally with the broad American questions that this policy raised.

Hay rebuffs Drago

This was the atmosphere prevailing at Washington when Drago's note of December 1902 arrived. In order to understand why Washington received the note coolly, as it did,[15] let us look more closely at the contents and implications of the note.

The greater part of it was devoted to an explanation of Drago's policy proposal. Two points in the explanation are of special interest to us. First, Drago spoke of the Monroe Doctrine with warm approval and quoted its warning to Europe not to interfere with or oppress the independent nations of America. He then went on at greater length to show how, as a result of developments since Monroe's day, the threat from Europe to America had taken a new form against which new

[14] Dexter Perkins, *Monroe Doctrine, 1867–1907*, p. 192.

[15] Drago complained that Secretary Hay's reply "en realidad parece haber tomado poco en cuenta los términos de nuestra comunicación." He blamed this partly on an error in the English translation of the note of December 29 prepared and transmitted by the Argentine minister in Washington (Drago, *op. cit.*, II, 56–58); but he was to find that in fact this had had little if any bearing on the attitude of the United States.

safeguards must be found. The reference here was to the new imperialism of Europe and to its use of the opening wedge of economic and financial penetration, followed by armed intervention and territorial occupation. Warning of the imminent danger that this technique, already fully developed in other parts of the world, would now be applied to Latin America, Drago wrote:

In recent times, there has been a marked tendency on the part of European publicists and in various expressions of European opinion to designate these [Latin American] countries as a suitable field for future territorial expansion. Thinkers of the first rank have indicated the desirability of turning in this direction the great efforts which the principal powers of Europe have hitherto devoted to the conquest of barren regions that have an unfavorable climate and lie in the remotest parts of the world. Already many European writers are pointing to rich, fertile South America as the theater in which the great powers, which have the instruments and arms of conquest already prepared, must necessarily wage their contest for power in the course of this century. . . . And it will not be denied [he continued] that the simplest way for the European governments to go about making seizures and supplanting local authorities is precisely through financial interventions; there are many examples to prove this.[16]

The note then proceeded to set forth Drago's substantive proposal for guarding against this danger by establishing the principle mentioned at the beginning of this essay, namely, that the collection of a public debt through armed intervention in an American nation or occupation of its territory, by a European power, be prohibited. The American nations, said Drago, should first adopt this principle among themselves and then seek to obtain the assent of the European nations to it.

The chief features of the Drago Doctrine were, therefore,

[16] This is my own translation of the Spanish text in Drago, *op. cit.*, II, 53.

as follows: First, it was based squarely upon the Western Hemisphere idea and made explicit reference to the Monroe Doctrine, which it was intended to supplement in order to guard against a type of threat from Europe which did not exist when Monroe's pronouncement was made. Second, it was offered as a regional American policy, not, as the forty-year-old Calvo Doctrine had been, as an amendment to general international law. Third, it proposed to make the rule of nonintervention absolute in the cases to which it applied. Fourth, and finally, it was to be implemented by multilateral, inter-American action.

Drago's proposal has been described above as intended to supplement the Monroe Doctrine. It was apparently not until the following year that he explicitly stated his intention in these terms,[17] but a careful reading of the note of December 1902 shows beyond reasonable doubt that the later statement represents not an afterthought but a clarification of his original thought. Consequently, the true character of his proposal would be made clearer if it were called not the Drago Doctrine but the Drago corollary to the Monroe Doctrine.

From the point of view of the pontiffs on the Potomac, the Drago Doctrine had the great merit of proclaiming the hemispheric faith and the fatal defect of making the political interpretation of that faith multilateral. The defect was fatal because Drago tied his proposal to the Monroe Doctrine. If, as seems likely, he expected Washington to be disposed kindly toward his proposal for this reason, he could hardly have been more mistaken. Not only was his proposed extension of the Monroe Doctrine multilateral, but if it were agreed to

[17] *Ibid.*, II, 74–75, preface to *La Argentina y el caso de Venezuela,* dated July 19, 1903. See also *ibid.*, p. 84: "la proposición de Monroe, a la cual nuestra doctrina viene a dar un 'concepto extensivo.'" In 1914 Drago described his doctrine as "algo como un corolario de la Doctrina Monroe: la Doctrina de Monroe financiera . . . ahi reside su originalidad: ha completado la doctrina de Monroe" (Silva, *op. cit.*, p. 507).

by the United States, its tendency would be to lead retro-actively to the multilateralization of Monroe's original pro-nouncement. This was something that the United States had always opposed, maintaining that the Monroe Doctrine was nothing if not a unilateral, national policy of the United States. As a heretic is worse than an infidel, Drago was to be shown no mercy on this point.

Diplomatic good manners, which were still observed in those days, forbade an open rebuff; and common sense for-bade a rebuff to one of the few Argentine statesmen who had ever spoken in praise of the Monroe Doctrine as if he meant it. Still more important, the United States was much con-cerned in the next few years with the question to which Drago's proposal was addressed, namely, how to curb Euro-pean intervention in America. Washington's problem was to purge Drago's idea of its multilateral implications as an inter-American doctrine, to refashion it in this respect according to its own unilateral specifications, and yet in doing so to give as little offense as possible to those with different views, such as the great powers of Europe, isolationists and internation-alists in the United States, and Drago himself.

Whether or not the problem was consciously formulated in these terms, it was solved in three stages during the next five years. The first step was taken when, in February 1903,[18] Secretary of State Hay replied to Drago's note in noncom-mittal terms. "Without expressing either agreement or dis-agreement" with Drago's proposal (to quote Hay's own words), he referred him to President Roosevelt's recent mes-sages and other public addresses for a statement of the United States' position on the general issue involved. According to the Cuban jurist Bustamente y Sirvén, Hay's note proves that

[18] Department of State, *Papers Relating to the Foreign Relations of the United States, 1903* (Washington, D.C., 1904), pp. 5–6. See pp. 1–5 for an English translation of Drago's note.

he did not at first appreciate the extraordinary significance of Drago's proposal, nor foresee the repercussions it was to have.[19] Though this explanation seems rather unlikely in view of Hay's knowledge and experience, it gains some support from the fact that Roosevelt's letters for this period make no mention of Drago's proposal, though they contain numerous references to the Venezuela crisis.[20]

A two-part settlement of the crisis was soon reached: the claims against Venezuela were submitted to arbitration and the question whether the claims of the three intervening powers (Germany, Britain, and Italy) were entitled to priority over those of the other claimant powers was submitted to the Hague Court. Early in 1904 the latter decided this question in the affirmative, thus not only giving explicit sanction to intervention but putting a premium upon it.[21] This decision, together with the imminent threat of another European intervention in America, this time in the Dominican Republic, made it impossible for the United States government to defer any longer a decision on the general policy question.

Accordingly, in December 1904, the United States took the second step by coming forward with a doctrine of its own, the Roosevelt corollary to the Monroe Doctrine. Like Monroe's original proposition, this corollary was embodied in the President's annual message to Congress. It was mainly the work of Secretary of War Elihu Root,[22] who a few months later was to succeed Hay as Secretary of State. In December 1905, again counseled by Root, Roosevelt returned to the subject and stated the corollary in its definitive form.

There were important resemblances as well as differences

[19] Drago, *op. cit.*, I, 35.

[20] Theodore Roosevelt, *The Letters,* ed. by Elting E. Morison, vol. III (Cambridge, Mass., 1951).

[21] Bemis, *Latin American Policy,* p. 151.

[22] Bartlett, *op. cit.*, p. 539; Philip C. Jessup, *Elihu Root* (New York, 1938), I, 470.

between Roosevelt's corollary to the Monroe Doctrine and Drago's. Both were addressed to the same general problem (European intervention in America) and were based upon the same assumptions (the Western Hemisphere idea and the Monroe Doctrine). Both proposed to solve the problem by making an exception to general international law in favor of the Western Hemisphere, and both proposed to achieve this solution by an American policy pronouncement, not through a universally agreed amendment to international law. But here Roosevelt parted company with Drago by proposing to implement this new policy in a totally different way (not through multilateral, inter-American action, but through unilateral action by the United States) and with totally different results: instead of abolishing intervention in the Western Hemisphere, Roosevelt explicitly sanctioned this practice and claimed for the United States a monopoly of the right to engage in it. Finally, whereas Drago had confined his proposal to forcible intervention for the collection of a public debt, the Roosevelt corollary applied to intervention of all kinds and for whatever purpose. To quote the broad and plain language of Roosevelt's first statement of it in 1904:

Chronic wrongdoing, or an impotence which results in a general loosening of the ties of civilized society, may in America, as elsewhere, ultimately require intervention by some civilized nation, and in the Western Hemisphere the adherence of the United States to the Monroe Doctrine may force the United States, however reluctantly, in flagrant cases of such wrongdoing or impotence, to the exercise of an international police power.

This was reinterpreting the Western Hemisphere idea with a vengeance. To be sure, the old, familiar idea of a regional American system was still there and along with it the even older antithesis of America versus Europe. But the corollary gave an entirely new twist to the relationship of the members

100

of the American system to one another by claiming for the United States the right of a general "international police power" throughout the Western Hemisphere. While this was described in terms of obligation rather than of right or privilege, an obligation that would be exercised only in "flagrant cases of wrongdoing or impotence," nevertheless the United States reserved to itself the right both to carry out any intervention and to decide when a case was sufficiently flagrant to require intervention. This made the United States not only the policeman of the Western Hemisphere but its judge as well. One of its most sympathetic commentators, S. F. Bemis, has called this new policy one of "protective imperialism."

Denaturing the Drago Doctrine

Drago's proposal of 1902 to the United States thus got its long-postponed answer. This not only rejected his policy (by implication only—neither it nor his name was even mentioned) but replaced it with one of a wholly different tenor. Yet while they rejected it as policy, Roosevelt and Root went on to champion the transformation of Drago's proposal into international law, contrary to his intention, in the modified and conditional form in which it was adopted at the Hague Conference of 1907. This surprising development, the reasons for which will be explained more fully below, brought to a close the third and last stage of the procedure by which the United States escaped from the multilateral net woven by Drago out of the Hemisphere idea. This closing stage began at the Third Pan American Conference, held at Rio de Janeiro in 1906. Root was there,[23] though not as a delegate, but

[23] Root's famous speech at the Rio de Janeiro conference can be conveniently consulted in his *Latin America and the United States: Addresses* (Cambridge, Mass., 1917), pp. 6–11. Though he gave the Western Hemisphere idea a more restricted political application than Blaine had done and than Wilson and Lansing were to do, he did express it in such phrases as "the American continents" and "the American republics, engaged in the same great task, inspired by the same purpose, and professing the same principles," and

Drago, though appointed a member of the Argentine delegation, resigned when he read his instructions, in which his successor as head of the Argentine foreign office opposed the hemispheric character of the Drago Doctrine and took the position that it must be converted into international law of universal, not regional, application.

At the Rio de Janeiro Conference, the United States played a leading part in beginning the process of denaturing the Drago Doctrine which was completed the following year at the Hague. Ostensibly, the action taken at the Conference was noncommittal, for it merely referred the whole question to the Hague—which was what Secretary Root's instructions to the United States delegates directed them to propose. In effect, however, this action settled two of the three major questions raised by the Drago Doctrine and settled them adversely to Drago, for it meant that if anything at all came of the doctrine, it would be in the form of international law, not policy, and that the law would be universal, not hemispheric.

Then, at The Hague, where he served as a member of the Argentine delegation, Drago was defeated on the third point as well, when his absolute ban on intervention was made conditional. Here again the United States took a leading part in defeating him, for the convention on this subject finally adopted by the Hague Conference was based upon a resolution offered by General Horace Porter in the name of the United States delegation. In its final form, the convention required all claims to be submitted to arbitration; but it explicitly sanctioned intervention if arbitration were refused or the arbitral award frustrated. Though unavailingly, Drago resisted to the end this watering down of his doctrine as well as its conversion into general international law, for he never

in the contrast between "our free lands" and Europe with its "burden of . . . armaments . . . massed behind [its] frontiers."

wavered in his contention that his doctrine was nothing if not an exclusively inter-American policy.[24]

Nevertheless, as Drago gazed sadly on the mangled remains of his five-year-old brain child, he expressed no resentment against the United States for the mayhem it had committed. On the contrary, he seems to have come out of the long ordeal with the same liking that he had had for the United States before it began. That he did so was due in no small measure to the diplomatic skill of Elihu Root. Root had definite ideas about the leading role that the United States must play in Western Hemisphere affairs; but so long as the Latin Americans would play the game according to his rules, he spared no pains to show the most exquisite consideration both in his regard for the national interests and susceptibilities of the Latin American countries and in his personal relations with their diplomatic representatives.[25] He anticipated by thirty years many of the measures and techniques of the Good Neighbor Policy and most of its fraternal liturgy. When he got down to business, Root's manner was quiet, simple, and disarming; and it was fatal to be disarmed by Root, for once his premises had been accepted, his logic was irresistible.

Root was remarkably successful in winning the friendship and confidence of the Latin Americans with whom he came in contact, even when the contact was brief and casual. Witness his tour of South America in 1906—the first visit ever made to that part of the world by an American Secretary of State—which was a personal triumph; forty years later he was still warmly remembered in the cities that he visited at that time. Witness also his long and fruitful friendship with the Brazilian Ambassador at Washington, Joaquim Nabuco.

It is not surprising, then, that Root was able to keep Drago happy while playing ducks and drakes with his doctrine. He

[24] Silva, *op. cit.,* p. 505.   [25] Jessup, *op. cit.,* I, 468–492.

was made to feel that while this needed to be touched up here and there and elsewhere, until it was unrecognizable, it had nevertheless won him a place in the front rank of contemporary statesmen. Root was in a sense the sponsor of Latin America at this Hague Conference. He was mainly responsible for getting all the countries of that area invited to it (only Mexico and Brazil had been invited to the first Hague conference) and for their playing an important part in it; Drago was one of the two most conspicuous Latin American delegates (the other being Ruy Barbosa of Brazil) and was appointed to the most important posts for which he was eligible.[26] Before the Conference and again at its close, Root transmitted an invitation to Drago to lecture at Harvard University and invited him to make his visit to the United States as an official guest of the government; only the pressure of business at home, we are told by his son, prevented his acceptance.[27]

The Hague convention also provided the United States with an escape from consequences of the Roosevelt corollary that might have proved embarrassing. If the ban on European intervention had been made absolute, the result might have been serious friction either with the great-power creditors or with the Latin American debtors or with both, unless the United States had assumed the unenviable role of bill collector for the Hemisphere.

So far as Britain was concerned, the danger of such friction seemed slight, though it is not entirely clear just what thoughts Downing Street had on the subject of bill collecting. At any rate, the British government was known to be friendly to the general purposes of the Roosevelt corollary and may even have had something to do with its adoption. Before that took place, Washington had received several indications from British sources that such a policy would be welcome to Downing Street. The most important indication of this kind

[26] Drago, *op. cit.*, I, 80–81.   [27] *Ibid.*, p. 50.

had been given by no less a person than Prime Minister Balfour in December 1902, at the height of the Venezuelan imbroglio. It was contained in a letter to Andrew Carnegie, who had passed it on to President Roosevelt and Secretary Hay at about the same time that they had received Argentine Foreign Minister Drago's note proposing his doctrine.[28] Balfour's suggestion had been brief but pregnant: Britain, he said, far from opposing the Monroe Doctrine, would be glad to see the United States take the troublesome Latin American republics in hand. Here was a clear sign that Britain was disposed to carry further that diplomatic retirement in favor of the United States which she had begun several years earlier.

This trend of British policy was obvious, and even Drago, in remote Argentina, had perceived its potential significance for the problem of intervention without knowing anything about Balfour's letter to Carnegie. In 1902 he had taken Britain's new respect for the Monroe Doctrine as one of the premises of his own doctrine, and a few years later he explained more fully why it had been one of his principal reasons for making his doctrine exclusively hemispheric. He wrote in 1906:

England has now officially accepted the Monroe Doctrine, very probably because it applies only to America. It is altogether likely that she would continue to oppose any effort to prevent her colonizing other parts of the world. It is possible that, in like manner, she might agree to a ban on forcible debt collection by European powers in America, though certainly not elsewhere.[29]

Some of the continental powers, however, were not so complaisant about banning European intervention in America. They regarded it as a great concession on their part even to let the United States join with them in their collection of Latin American debts. An arrangement of this kind, a joint

[28] Bemis, *Latin American Policy*, p. 153.   [29] Drago, *op. cit.*, II, 82.

receivership in Santo Domingo, had been proposed to the United States government by some of them in November 1904, on the eve of President Roosevelt's first statement of his corollary. Washington had turned it down for fear that it might lead to the "Ottomanization" of Latin America.[30]

Yet it soon became obvious that a negative reply was not enough, for every creditor nation still remained free to determine for itself when intervention was justified and then call on the United States to make good under the Roosevelt corollary. The question, already urgent, was likely to become more so, given the rapid rate at which the European economic penetration of Latin America was proceeding and the unstable if not chaotic condition of several of the Latin American countries.

The answer was provided by the Hague convention of 1907, which, without closing the door to intervention, took the decision as to the need for it out of the hands of the interested parties and subjected it to a process which would screen and delay potential interventions and thereby greatly reduce pressure on the corollary from this source.

It was thus through an amendment to general international law that the United States got out of the corner into which it had maneuvered itself by brushing aside Drago's multilateral corollary to the Monroe Doctrine in favor of its own unilateral corollary. The latter, however, still remained intact as a kind of second line of defense, an ultimate policy statement which could be invoked at Washington's will if the global Hague system did not work out in the Western Hemisphere to Washington's satisfaction.

The developments described in this chapter make an extraordinary story in more ways than one. In a play started by Foreign Minister Drago of Argentina, the United States took the ball away from him and ran for a touchdown and

[30] Bemis, *Latin American Policy*, p. 153.

yet contrived to make him feel when the game was over that he had been on the winning team. In the process, the United States, profiting by a favorable turn of British policy, gave an entirely new twist to the Western Hemisphere idea by quite plausibly converting it into a doctrine of Yankee hegemony. At first, in the Roosevelt corollary, Washington overreached itself, but it then regained its balance at the Hague by shedding the most vexatious of its recently assumed responsibilities in the Western Hemisphere. But it still kept a firm grip on the hemispheric authority which it had assumed in the Roosevelt corollary, so that the world was now presented with the singular spectacle of a hemispheric agglomeration of twenty-one nominally independent nations falling under the hegemony of one of them in a regional system which had found that it had to rely upon a global agency for the settlement of one of its most troublesome questions.

The singularity of this spectacle caused no loss of sleep in Washington, where at the end of 1907 there was a feeling of solid satisfaction with the nation's performance during the previous ten years in its new role of a world power. Europe, too, was reasonably well satisfied with the performance. The United States had by this time developed a capitalist-industrial society of the same general type as that which had already grown up in the larger European states. As a result, the leaders in Washington and those in Western Europe came to understand each other better and better as time went on. The same development, however, widened the already considerable gap between Anglo-Saxon America and Latin America.

VI

Whose Hemisphere?

IN THE quarter century from the first pronouncement of the Roosevelt corollary in 1904 to the beginning of the Great Depression in 1929, two major trends in inter-American relations raised the question of Western Hemisphere unity in a way that suggests a comparison with the Babylonian captivity and the Great Schism of the late Middle Ages.

The first was a trend toward the hegemony of the United States in Western Hemisphere affairs, a hegemony based upon an increasing preponderance of power—naval, economic, and political—deliberately exercised in accordance with the new concept of the civilizing mission of the United States in the New World. As many Latin Americans saw it, the result was to place the Pan American movement in a dependent relation to Washington rather like that in which the papacy had stood with regard to the French monarchy when certain fourteenth-century popes lived in "Babylonian captivity" at Avignon.

108

The second trend was stimulated by a reaction against the first. In twentieth-century America, as in fourteenth-century Europe, the subordination of an international institution to a single nation provoked mounting resentment and schismatic tendencies among the rest. In America these reached their climax at the Fifth Pan American Conference, held at Havana in 1928, and turned that meeting into a fiasco which gave warning that the loose-knit Pan American family might disintegrate completely if grievances were not redressed.

Colossus of the Western Hemisphere

First let us look at the Babylonian captivity—the growth of the power of the United States in the Western Hemisphere in this quarter-century, the use that was made of it, and the conception of hemispheric relations that underlay this.

An examination of the unfolding power situation properly begins with sea power, for in the communications of the United States with Latin America in the preair age, sea power was decisive. This fact was vividly illustrated by a chain of events that began, on the very eve of the period we are considering, with the secession of Panama from Colombia (in 1903).[1] Though it was impossible for troops from the loyal Colombian mainland to reach the infected Isthmian area by land, they could have reached it by sea; but the United States Navy prevented all but one battalion from doing so, and as a result the Panamanians won their independence in the twinkling of an eye. The United States recognized their independence no less quickly and then went on to negotiate with the new Republic of Panama a treaty which made it a satellite of the Union and opened the way for the construction of a fortified Panama Canal. The way for its fortification had already been cleared by the Hay-Pauncefote Treaty of

[1] Dwight C. Miner, *The Fight for the Panama Route* (New York, 1940), ch. x, "Revolution in Panama."

1901 with an obliging British government. Completed and opened to traffic in 1914, the fortified Panama Canal was at once the chief prop and the clearest symbol of the revolution in sea power that had taken place in the Caribbean in the previous two decades—the replacement of British control by the unchallenged and unchallengeable domination of the United States.[2] What is more, by 1914 the preponderance thus firmly established in the Caribbean area had made it possible for the United States to exercise effective control of the high seas throughout the Western Hemisphere.

The year 1914 may therefore be taken as marking the completion of the first stage in the rise of the United States to hemispheric sea power, but an examination of the four major factors that had produced this rise shows that south of the Caribbean it did not yet rest on a firm foundation. Two of these factors might be presumed to be constant, as in fact they proved to be. One was the will of the people and government of the United States to build and maintain an ever-increasing navy. This they did, with some fluctuations but no major interruptions, from the 1890's until, in the 1920's, the world situation seemed to justify a relaxation. The other was the advantage which the United States enjoyed over Europe in naval operations in American waters as a result of the late nineteenth-century development of the iron-clad, steam-propelled warship. This change greatly increased the fighting strength of warships within their radius of action, but it also greatly reduced this radius by the rigid requirements of fuel and service which it imposed.[3] No major variation in this factor seemed likely in 1914, and in fact none occurred until a quarter-century later, in World War II.

But a scrutiny of the other two major factors gave no cause

---

[2] Harold and Margaret Sprout, *Toward a New Order of Sea Power, 1918–1922* (New York, 1940), p. 26.

[3] *Ibid.,* p. 25.

for complacency in the Washington of 1914. These factors were interlocking: one was the friendly diplomatic and naval retirement of Great Britain in favor of the United States which began in 1896 and which has already been noticed in the preceding essay, and the other was the increasingly tense balance-of-power situation in Europe, which was partly responsible for Britain's more conciliatory attitude toward the United States. After 1900, we are told, this tension repeatedly frustrated her imperial ambitions in America as well as other parts of the world and led to a greater and greater concentration of the British fleet in European waters. The same was true of her chief rival, Germany, and the big new German navy. As a result, after about 1900 the rivalry of these two powers canceled both of them out so far as sea power in America was concerned—to the great benefit and relief of the United States. The eminent American naval strategist and historian Alfred Thayer Mahan took note of this European balance-of-power situation frequently, and always with solid satisfaction; and in 1910 he stressed the fact that the mutual antagonism between Britain and Germany chained the two strongest fleets in the world to European waters "in peace as well as war." [4]

This situation, so happy from Washington's point of view, was rendered almost ideal in 1914 by the opening of the fortified Panama Canal; but one of its essential conditions was destroyed by World War I, which broke out just as the canal was opened. The war ended in the annihilation of the German navy and a reduction in the relative strength of the French navy, so that by 1919 Britain was once more, for the first time since 1900, without a serious European rival for sea power. In the meantime, however, the United States had undertaken and was rapidly carrying out a gigantic naval construction program. It thereby in effect provided from its

[4] *Ibid.*, p. 24.

own resources a substitute for that prewar balance-of-power rivalry in Europe which had for a time given it national protection and Hemisphere preponderance at a bargain price. The British Admiralty was, understandably, reluctant to accept the logic of a situation which seemed in some of its major outlines so painfully like the one that Britain had just fought a successful war to liquidate.

How this potentially dangerous problem in Anglo-American relations resisted successful settlement at the Paris Peace Conference of 1919 and was finally solved only after an interval of more than two years, at the Washington Conference of 1921–1922,[5] are questions we cannot enter into here. Suffice it to say that one of the major agreements reached by this latter conference crystallized the new order of sea power based upon regional distribution, which since 1900 had gradually supplanted the old nineteenth-century order of world sea power concentrated in Britannia's hands. She was still mistress of the seas in the eastern Atlantic, the North Sea, and other areas; but Japan was now accorded this role in the western Pacific, and the United States in the Western Hemisphere. As a result, so far as sea power was concerned, the position of the United States in the Western Hemisphere had never been stronger—nor, conversely, had the rest of the Western Hemisphere ever been in a weaker position vis-à-vis the United States—than in the last seven years of the period with which we are concerned in this essay, namely, the seven years from the end of the Washington Conference to the beginning of the Great Depression in 1929.

By an interesting coincidence—perhaps it was nothing more than that—these years also saw the greatest outburst of United States investment in South America that had ever taken place, and one of the greatest that has ever occurred in a comparable period anywhere in the world. In 1924 United

[5] *Ibid.*, *passim*, especially pp. 61–66, on "the naval battle of Paris."

States investments in South America already amounted to the tidy sum of $1,411,000,000; by 1929 they had more than doubled, amounting at the end of that year to $3,014,000,000. Though the volume of American investments was larger in Canada and Europe than in Latin America, the rate of increase in the former areas in the same five years was considerably lower—about 35 per cent in the case of Canada and 75 per cent in that of Europe.[6]

The rapid penetration of South America by United States capital was particularly important because, before 1924, the Latin American investments of the United States had been concentrated mainly in Middle America. Even there they had been built up almost entirely in the past quarter-century. In 1897 the total for all Latin America was only $308,000,000; of this Mexico alone accounted for $200,000,000, or nearly two thirds, and Cuba and the other West Indies came next, with $49,000,000, leaving only $69,000,000, or less than 25 per cent, for all Central and South America. By 1929 the Latin American total had increased nearly eighteenfold, to $5,430,-000,000; and South America alone accounted for over half of this huge investment. Only Great Britain still led the United States in the field of Latin American investments. No other competitor remotely approached these two; and not only was Britain's lead narrow, but most of her investments were concentrated in southern South America, and above all in a single country, Argentina.

In the foreign trade of Latin America, the progress made by the United States after 1914 was still more impressive, for in this respect it drew far ahead of Britain as well as all other competitors. Though it was aided in doing so by the wartime dislocation of European trade from 1914 to 1918, the

[6] Data on investments in this paragraph and the next were drawn from Cleona Lewis, *America's Stake in International Investments* (Washington, D.C., 1938), p. 606. See also Max Winkler, *Investments of United States Capital in Latin America* (Boston, 1928).

process was already manifestly under way before the war began. One factor was the growth of investments, which had increased fivefold between 1897 and 1914. Another was the establishment of Latin American branches of United States national banks, which was first made possible by the Federal Reserve Act of 1913. There had also been by 1914 a considerable improvement in shipping facilities and cable communications.

Nevertheless, it was only after 1914 that most of these factors came into full play. Thus, in the next ten years United States–owned cable mileage in Latin American waters increased from 14,000 to 38,000, while European-owned mileage declined slightly from its prewar figure of 25,000. Partly as a result of this, United States news services, which had played a minor role in Latin America before 1914, were by 1924 supplying its newspapers with most of their foreign news, and a larger part of this than ever before related to the United States.[7] All this was gratifying to the latter's national pride, but by 1925 one of its writers who took a sympathetic view of this wave of expansion was warning: "As the stronger state—as the creditor state—we must be prepared to be suspected and hated in many South American circles even if we behave well." [8]

The civilizing mission

And how was the United States behaving? While its government and people were building up its naval and economic preponderance in the New World in the manner just described, they were also developing a new concept of the role

[7] Julius Klein, "Economic Rivalries in Latin America," *Foreign Affairs,* III (1924), 242–243. Topically arranged information on many aspects of the early stage of this multiplication of the United States' contacts with Latin America will be found in William Spence Robertson, *Hispanic American Relations with the United States* (New York, 1923).

[8] Herbert Feis, "The Export of American Capital," *Foreign Affairs,* III (1925), 681.

their country ought to play in relation to its southern neighbors. Until about 1920 this can be summed up in the term "civilizing mission," which connoted unilateral action, both political and economic, supported by missionary zeal and, if necessary, by armed force as well. After 1920, while there was no abrupt break, there was a sharp decline both of missionary zeal and of confidence in any unilateral approach to hemispheric problems.

With one brief exception, however, the Western Hemisphere idea in one form or another dominated both public opinion and government action in the field of United States foreign policy throughout this quarter-century. The exception consisted in the frustrated experiment with universalism and the League of Nations from 1916 to 1920 under the leadership of Woodrow Wilson, but the net result of that episode was to provoke a reaction in favor of the Hemisphere idea.

The concept of the civilizing mission of the United States took shape in the first decade of the century and received its classic formulation in Herbert Croly's widely read book, *The Promise of American Life,* published in 1909.[9] Croly's book has a special interest for us because it was produced by the fusion of the Western Hemisphere idea with the idea of Manifest Destiny. This was a development which could hardly have been foreseen in the mid-nineteenth century, when, as noted in an earlier essay, the two ideas were mutually antagonistic, if not mutually exclusive. Thus, during the first grand climacteric of Manifest Destiny in the 1840's, that term meant continental expansion to the Pacific, largely at the expense of one of the sister republics of America. By 1900, however, the process of continental expansion had long since

[9] On this subject I am much indebted to the excellent article by William E. Leuchtenburg, "Progressivism and Imperialism: The Progressive Movement and American Foreign Policy, 1898–1916," in *Mississippi Valley Historical Review,* XXXIX (1952), 483–504.

been completed and the great majority of the people of the United States of all shades of opinion were agreed that their country did not need and should not take any more territory in the Western Hemisphere, except a few feet here and there for a Panama Canal or a Guantánamo naval base.

But new forces were now at work in the United States which produced a new form of expansionism. Added to the determination, which grew so rapidly in the 1890's, to take a more active part in world affairs was the conviction that the United States had a unique contribution to make to the betterment of the world. It could not only do as much for backward peoples as any other civilized nation and do it better; it was also uniquely qualified to confer upon those who should in time become worthy of it the ultimate boon of democracy. This was a new kind of Manifest Destiny. It obviously had global implications, but it was oriented mainly toward Latin America by the ingrained hemispheric habit of thought. Thus the civilizing mission was first and foremost a mission to be performed in Latin America.

Obviously, there was a close connection between this notion of a civilizing mission and the protective imperialism represented by the Roosevelt corollary. Indeed, the former was an outgrowth of the latter—Croly's book, published five years after the corollary, makes that unmistakably clear. But the point to be stressed is that the outgrowth was in fact a growth, an extension; for while the civilizing mission subsumed and strongly reaffirmed protective imperialism, including specifically armed intervention in Latin America, it contemplated an intervention of a much broader, deeper, and more lasting kind. Protective imperialism would intervene to correct situations of chronic wrongdoing and chaos only to the extent necessary to prevent European intervention and would then withdraw. The civilizing mission, on the other hand, had no such *ad hoc* character or limited objective. The missionary's work is not done when the devils have been cast out; it has hardly begun. He must stay on until he has taught his charges how to lead the good life, and that may take quite a long time.

All this had highly important implications for hemispheric relations, and these were brought out clearly in Croly's book of 1909. The first task of a truly national policy, he wrote, was to develop hemispheric solidarity within a "stable American international system." He then went on to describe how this was to be achieved:

In all probability no American international system will ever be established without the forcible pacification of one or more centers of disorder. . . . Any international American system might have to undertake a task in states like Venezuela, similar to that which the United States is performing in Cuba [where the United States intervened under the Platt Amendment for three years, 1906–1909]. . . . The United States has already made an effective beginning in this great work, both by the pacification of Cuba and by the attempt to introduce a little order into the affairs of the turbulent Central American republics.[10]

To be sure, Croly proposed that the United States carry forward this "great work" on the basis of inter-American cooperation. But given the great disparity of strength between the United States and the other American republics, there could be no doubt as to which of them would have the guid-

[10] *Ibid.*, pp. 501–502. For earlier and broader discussions of the background, see Ralph H. Gabriel, *The Course of American Democratic Thought* (New York, 1940), ch. xxvi, "The 'Mission of America' in the Progressive Era"; Merle Curti, *The Growth of American Thought* (New York, 1943), ch. xxvi, "America Recrosses the Oceans," especially pp. 659–675; and Richard Hofstadter, *Social Darwinism in American Thought, 1860–1915* (Philadelphia, 1945), ch. ix, "Racism and Imperialism." See also the works cited in Essay V, note 9. Cf. Dexter Perkins, *The American Approach to Foreign Policy* (Uppsala and Stockholm, 1949), ch. ii, "Is There an American Imperialism?"

ing hand in an enterprise admittedly based upon the use of force.

Croly and his fellow Progressives were in fact strong supporters of imperialism during their most flourishing period, from about 1905 to 1915. That was paradoxical, for it seemed in headlong conflict with their domestic policy, which was one of reform in the interest of social welfare and justice and at the expense of predatory capitalism. Actually, as they saw it, there was no such conflict; on the contrary, an imperialist foreign policy would give positive support to their domestic reforms by breaking down the prevalent Jeffersonian, laissez-faire tradition. This would facilitate the revival of the Hamiltonian tradition and that extension of the area of government control over the economic and social life of the nation which the Progressives' domestic program required. In other words, they were interventionists abroad because they wanted to be interventionists at home. Note the satisfaction with which Herbert Croly described this process:

Not until the end of the Spanish War [of 1898] was a condition of public feeling created, which made it possible to revive Hamiltonianism. That war and its resulting policy of extra-territorial expansion, so far from hindering the process of domestic amelioration, availed, from the sheer force of the national aspirations it aroused, to give a tremendous impulse to the work of national reform . . . and it indirectly helped to place in the Presidential chair the man who . . . represented both the national idea and the spirit of reform.[11]

That man was, of course, Theodore Roosevelt. First and foremost a nationalist, Roosevelt stepped into the leadership of Progressivism after it had developed from a movement into a national party (in 1912). He was able to do this the more easily because he shared many other assumptions of the Progressives besides their Hamiltonian creed. Among the

[11] Leuchtenburg, *op. cit.*, p. 502.

118

most important of these for the development of the Progressives' Western Hemisphere imperialism was a belief in the supremacy of the white race, more specifically the Anglo-Saxon race, and in the duty of the United States to help carry the "white man's burden."

Clearly, the Anglo-Saxon white man had a heavy burden to carry in Latin America, where the only whites were "decadent" Latins, and the majority of the population were Indians, Negroes, or (worst of all, according to racist doctrine) mixed races. And, of course, under the Monroe Doctrine, the white man's burden in that part of the world would have to be carried by the United States. The temper of the Progressives in this matter was foreshadowed as early as 1898 by one of their first and most influential leaders, Albert J. Beveridge, the eloquent young senator from Indiana. Advocating the annexation of Cuba and Puerto Rico, Beveridge brushed aside impatiently the objections that to rule those peoples without their consent would be contrary to the principles of the United States' own Declaration of Independence and that in any case they could never form a natural part of the United States since they were not contiguous:

The proposition of the opposition [snorted Beveridge] makes the Declaration of Independence preposterous, like the reading of Job's lamentations would be at a wedding. . . . I answer, the rule of liberty, that all just governments derive their authority from the consent of the governed, applies only to those who are capable of self-government. Cuba not contiguous? Porto Rico not contiguous? . . . Our navy will make them contiguous! [12]

So far, we have been speaking only of the Progressives; but by 1910 the idea of the civilizing mission which underlay their imperialism had permeated the other two major political groups as well—the "Old Guard" conservatives who now

[12] Claude G. Bowers, *Beveridge and the Progressive Era* (Boston, 1932), pp. 73–76.

controlled the Republican party and also the Democratic party which was soon to come to power under the leadership of Woodrow Wilson through the presidential election of 1912. About 1900 the conservative Republicans had opposed imperialism, in America as elsewhere. Now they supported it—not so much the booted-and-spurred imperialism of a Beveridge or a Roosevelt, but rather the milder variety known as Dollar Diplomacy. First fully developed and given this name during the administration of President Taft and his Secretary of State Philander C. Knox, a Pennsylvania corporation lawyer, this device for the financial and economic penetration and control of backward countries was applied on a considerable scale only in Latin America. It was pictured as not a selfish but a noble policy, which would help the Latin Americans to raise their standard of living and their standard of political behavior and ultimately to achieve internal order and democracy à la Uncle Sam, substituting ballots for bullets in the settlement of their political disputes.[13] This may have been mere rationalization, but it was rationalization in terms of the civilizing mission and the Hemisphere idea.

Wilson: From regionalism to universalism

As for Woodrow Wilson, who occupied the White House for the next eight years (1913–1921), the civilizing mission is one of the chief clues to a mystery which has puzzled many students of his Latin American policy—the contradiction between his liberal principles and his imperialistic practices.[14]

[13] Arthur P. Whitaker, "From Dollar Diplomacy to the Good Neighbor Policy," *Inter-American Economic Affairs*, IV (1951), 13–15.

[14] After the foregoing was written, I was happy to find confirmation of this view in Arthur S. Link, *Woodrow Wilson and the Progressive Era, 1910–1917* (New York, 1954), in which the first chapter on Wilson's foreign policy bears the title "Missionary Diplomacy." The reader is referred particularly to the paragraph on p. 82 beginning "The missionary impulse helps to explain much that is baffling about Wilson's foreign policy. . . ." Important information about William Jennings Bryan's role in 1913–1915 is contained in Selig

What has not been so often noticed is the fact that Wilson also made two striking and mutually contradictory contributions to the history of the Western Hemisphere idea, which he first exalted as never before and then abased to the point of extinction. Interesting in themselves, these contradictory developments are deserving of attention here because of their bearing upon the Hemisphere idea, and because, as will be shown in the next two essays, they were repeated in the same order after 1933.

Wilson came into office in 1913 promising a new deal in foreign as well as domestic policy. He began by denouncing imperialism and by repudiating Dollar Diplomacy and intervention; he applied these principles specifically to Latin America in his notable Mobile Address of October 1913, in which he assured the southern neighbors that the United States would henceforth treat them as equals. Yet in the end he carried out more armed interventions in Latin America than Roosevelt and Taft combined, revived and extended Dollar Diplomacy, and developed still another form of intervention by changing the United States' recognition policy from *de facto* to constitutional.

In Wilson's own mind, however, there was no inconsistency between his principles and his practice, for with him the overriding principle was the responsibility of power. The United States had now acquired so great a preponderance of power in the Western Hemisphere that it had not only the right but the duty to intervene in other American states in the performance of its civilizing mission.

Intervention, however, was not the only alternative considered, for the whole question of Western Hemisphere relations was re-examined during his first term. The climate of opinion favored the inquiry. Outside government circles, a

Adler, "Bryan and Wilsonian Caribbean Penetration," *Hispanic American Historical Review*, XX (1940), 198–226.

sign of the times was the publication in 1913 of Hiram Bingham's *The Monroe Doctrine: An Obsolete Shibboleth,* which argued that that unilateral doctrine had outlived its usefulness and become an incitement to Yankeephobia and that the establishment of a new relationship of inter-American reciprocity was overdue. A member of Wilson's official family, Robert Lansing, then counselor for the Department of State, wrote to somewhat the same effect, though in much more measured terms, in a memorandum of June 11, 1914.[15] Lansing distinguished sharply between the unilateral Monroe Doctrine, with its claim to primacy, and multilateral Pan Americanism, with its basic principle of juridical equality. Pointing out, as Drago had done (though without mentioning him or his proposal), that foreign economic penetration of Latin America had created a danger against which the Monroe Doctrine provided no defense, he urged a redefinition of the latter to meet the new danger and to serve the interests not only of the United States but of all the American states. The new policy, he concluded, should be based on "more altruistic and humanitarian principles, which will be in harmony with the sense of fraternal responsibility, which is increasingly dominant in all our international relations."

By November 1915 Lansing had swung around to the support of widespread unilateral intervention in the Caribbean danger zone and had abandoned humanitarianism as an argument, though not as a purpose. "The argument based on humanitarian purpose," he explained, "does not appeal to me, even though it might be justly urged, because too many international crimes have been committed in the name of humanity." [16] For the Hemisphere as a whole, he nevertheless

[15] Department of State, *The Lansing Papers, 1914–1920* (Washington, 1940), II, 460–465.

[16] *Ibid.*, 466–467, Secretary of State Lansing to President Wilson, November 24, 1915.

continued to urge a Pan American policy based on principles of equality and reciprocity, as in his address to the Pan American Scientific Congress on December 27, 1915. A week later his young relative John Foster Dulles followed this with an address in the same vein, though with even stronger multilateral implications. Both addresses have already been cited in the opening essay as expressions of the Western Hemisphere idea.

While World War I led to further interventions, it also for a time promoted Pan Americanism. Combined with the other factors just noted, it produced the first of Wilson's two innovations in the political application of the Western Hemisphere idea. This was the Pan American Pact which he drafted in conference with his close adviser, Colonel E. M. House, in December 1914, and then took up with various Latin American governments in January 1915.[17] The most important of the Pact's four articles was the first, which provided that "the high contracting parties . . . hereby join one another in a common and mutual guarantee of territorial integrity and of political independence under republican forms of government." This, together with the other articles (on the settlement of boundary disputes, control of the export of arms, and suppression of revolutionary expeditions from one country against the government of another), envisaged the creation of a true regional security system in America.

The general idea of the pact was as old as Bolívar, and its

[17] Bemis, *Latin American Policy*, pp. 194–197. As Bemis points out, the idea of the pact originated not with House but with another Texan, Representative James L. Slayden. A more detailed analysis of the genesis of this pact and its epilogue is contained in Malbone W. Graham, *American Diplomacy in the International Community* (Baltimore, 1948), Appendix IV, pp. 162–174. Link, *op. cit.*, p. 106, believes that "the historian must be allowed a few doubts as to the administration's sincerity in proposing it [the Pan American Pact]." See also Harley Notter, *The Origins of the Foreign Policy of Woodrow Wilson* (Baltimore, 1937).

123

revival at this time was due to a familiar motivation—that combined fear of European aggression and the desire to widen the gap between the "hemisphere of peace" and the broils of Europe which had from the outset been a chief component of the Western Hemisphere idea. What was novel was that now for the first time the United States sponsored the idea and that in some respects Wilson carried it even further than Bolívar had done. From the point of view of the United States, Wilson's Pan American Pact was a startling innovation, for it was intended to multilateralize the hitherto jealously guarded Monroe Doctrine.

Though six of the smaller Latin American states signified their approval of the pact, it was not adopted. Chile opposed it because of a territorial dispute with Peru; Brazil held back out of deference to Chile; and Argentina's attitude, originally favorable, was reversed by a change of administration in 1916. The United States' own interventions in Mexico and the Caribbean countries were a further obstacle.[18]

After two years of futile effort on behalf of his pact, Wilson executed one of those changes of front which have so often made the foreign policy of the United States puzzling to its own people as well as to foreigners. In May 1916, little more than a year after first taking up the Pan American Pact with the Latin American neighbors, he came out strongly for a global association of nations, and after the middle of 1917 he dropped the Pan American Pact completely.[19] In Western Hemisphere affairs he reverted to a unilateralism as pronounced as Theodore Roosevelt's. Wilson was still the internationalist, more than ever the internationalist; but he seemed

[18] Link, *op. cit.*, p. 197.

[19] Graham, *op. cit.*, p. 134, dates the beginning of the shift earlier (January 1916), and states (p. 173) that "the final transit from a regional to a world-wide Covenant was made in Wilson's mind some time between June 9 . . . and July 29 [1918]." But evidence in *Lansing Papers*, II, 500 indicates that for all practical purposes the pact was discarded in May 1917.

to pride himself on having graduated from regionalism to universalism.

As many writers have pointed out, there is no necessary contradiction between these two types of international cooperation, but apparently Wilson thought there was. At any rate, the League of Nations Covenant of 1919, which represents his fully matured thought on the subject, made no reference whatever to the thirty-year-old Pan American system. It did make a reference to the Monroe Doctrine, thereby according a measure of recognition to the Western Hemisphere idea, but this was only because irresistible political pressure from home forced Wilson to get the Doctrine written into the Covenant. So distasteful did he find the task that he left the drafting of the passage to others. Many tried their hands at it. Midway in the months-long peace conference at the Hotel Crillon in Paris, one of the participants noted in his diary: "I am probably the only person in the Crillon who is not working on a draft of the [Monroe Doctrine] reservation. . . . And scores of people outside the Crillon are also working on drafts." [20] It was another case of too many cooks, for the reservation finally adopted inaccurately described the Monroe Doctrine as a "regional understanding." That was something it had never been; it had been only a unilateral policy of the United States. It is true that, according to Wilson, the Covenant was "but a confirmation and an extension of the Monroe Doctrine," [21] but to give the Doctrine world-wide extension was to negate the Western Hemisphere idea underlying it.

[20] Stephen Bonsal, *Unfinished Business* (New York, 1944), p. 150; Thomas A. Bailey, *Woodrow Wilson and the Lost Peace* (New York, 1945), pp. 214–218.

[21] Bonsal, *op. cit.*, p. 158, Bonsal's entry for March 25, 1919. On April 12, 1919, Wilson further assured the delegates that the Monroe Doctrine was "the real forerunner of the League of Nations," and asked rhetorically, "Indeed are we not assembled here to consecrate and extend the horizon of this document as a perpetual charter for all the world?" (*ibid.*, pp. 184–185).

"Pan Americanism is a living force"

After the defeat of Wilson and the League, the Hemisphere idea, unilaterally interpreted, resumed its sway in the United States and maintained it throughout the Republican Restoration of 1921–1933. Even Archibald Cary Coolidge (the historian, not the President), who was primarily interested in relations with Europe, recorded in 1927 that "Pan Americanism . . . is a living force today . . . [and] is popular with public opinion." [22] The Republican Restoration gave the Hemisphere idea a tone which was less minatory than that of the Big Stick era. Indeed, the first Secretary of State during this period, Charles Evans Hughes, aided for a time by Sumner Welles, began to liquidate imperialism and the interventions in the Caribbean area which constituted its most obvious expression. He also interpreted the Monroe Doctrine in such a way as to restore to it its earlier character as "solely a policy of self-defense" and made it what his latest biographer calls the foundation for a hemispheric policy of positive helpfulness.[23] He thus anticipated the Clark Memorandum of 1930 and, to a limited degree, the Good Neighbor Policy of the following decade.

Hughes also explicitly stated his belief in the existence of a special relationship among the American states:

There can be no doubt that there are Pan American interests and that there is a Pan American sentiment which demands the special cooperation of the American states. . . . Pan Americanism rests upon the solid fact of our neighborhood and intercourse. It is not simply for our generation, but for all time.[24]

[22] Archibald Cary Coolidge, "The Grouping of Nations," *Foreign Affairs,* V (1927), 182–183.

[23] Merlo J. Pusey, *Charles Evans Hughes* (New York, 1951), II, 531, 536–537.

[24] Charles Evans Hughes, *Our Relations to the Nations of the Western Hemisphere* (Princeton, 1928), pp. 117–118.

But his idea of hemispheric co-operation did not extend into the field of security. Wilson's Pan American Pact found no echo in his policy. The other American states were encouraged to adopt "Monroe Doctrines" of their own, but the Monroe Doctrine would be interpreted and applied by the United States in its own way.[25] In short, while Hughes thought in hemispheric terms, and while he acted benevolently in the special relationship implied by those terms, his policy was one of the lone hand; and so were the policies of his successors during the remainder of the Republican Restoration.

By this time enthusiasm for the militant civilizing mission had withered away, partly under the wintry blast of general disillusionment that swept over the United States as well as many other countries after the war and partly from distaste for the fruits of such missionary activity. Haiti illustrated the latter point. It was the scene of one of those police actions so much admired by Herbert Croly. In 1916 the United States Navy took over this little country and gave it the benefits of civilization under a constitution drawn up by no less a person than Franklin Delano Roosevelt, then Assistant Secretary of Navy; but the Haitian people did not co-operate fully, and an uprising was suppressed only after nearly 2,000 of them had been killed by the Marines. The Haitian affair was apparently the starting point of a complete reversal of the remnant of the Progressive party's attitude toward imperialism; henceforth the party was its sharpest critic.[26]

In the 1920's, however, the Progressives were a small and badly organized remnant, and the Republicans were in firm

[25] Pusey, op. cit., II, 535–536.

[26] E.g., Robert Morss Lovett, "American Foreign Policy: A Progressive View," Foreign Affairs, III (1924), 49–60, especially p. 52: "The difference between the Third Party movement of 1912 and that of today is at no point more striking than in the attitudes respectively taken toward the question of imperialism. The Progressives of 1912 blindly followed Roosevelt in his defense of a predatory policy of which he was one of the conspicuous exponents. But during the next four years the Progressives awoke."

control. The latter, too, abandoned the idea of the civilizing mission in the old form, but they produced a new edition of it bearing the imprint of the business ethos, which could be summarized in the proposition that business brings uplift, and uplift pays dividends. Yet business alone did not bear the whole burden; soldier, sailor, and diplomat were there to help—and they did. That they would do so more and more seemed to be indicated by President Coolidge's public assertion in 1927, apropos of a situation in Central America, that an American citizen and his property in a foreign country are a part of the national domain of the United States.[27] What this view had already meant for Latin America was shown by the fact that, according to a survey made in 1924, only six of the twenty Latin American republics were free from interference by the United States in one form or another, including official direction of financial policy, and in six interference was backed by the presence of armed forces.[28]

"We could not be Pan Americanists"

In these circumstances, Yankeephobia flourished in Latin America. At the very beginning of the century, it had been given a literary vogue by leading men of letters such as the Nicaraguan poet Rubén Darío and the Uruguayan essayist José Enrique Rodó. This vogue was kept alive by others such as the Mexican Carlos Pereyra and the Argentine Manuel Ugarte, whose book *The Destiny of a Continent* won continent-wide renown as the classic indictment of Yankee imperialism. As the economic penetration by the Yankees proceeded apace, Wall Street came to be as cordially detested by the generality of Latin Americans as it was by the farmers of the United States itself in William Jennings Bryan's day; but in Latin America, detestation was aggravated by grow-

[27] Bemis, *Latin American Policy*, p. 419, n. 15.
[28] Lovett, *op. cit.*, p. 51, citing a recent article by S. G. Inman.

ing nationalism. In 1922, at a banquet given in Buenos Aires for the distinguished Mexican Minister of Public Education, José Vasconcelos, the then even more distinguished Argentine sociologist José Ingenieros said:

We are not, we do not want to be any longer, we could not be Pan Americanists. The United States is to be feared because it is great, rich, and enterprising. What concerns us is to find out whether there is a possibility of balancing its power to the extent necessary to save our political independence and the sovereignty of our countries.

Moreover, the process of economic penetration had cost the United States much of the support it had formerly had among Latin American liberals. The latter were alienated by the unholy alliance, as they regarded it, between expanding Yankee business enterprise and the reactionary oligarchies in their own countries. Anti-imperialism flourished, and the United States was its principal target, as in the program of the APRA (American Popular Revolutionary Alliance), first formulated by the Peruvian Víctor Raúl Haya de la Torre in Mexico in 1924.[29] "Yankee imperialism" had become in effect a single word, like "damn Yankee" in the post-Civil-War South.

For our purpose, the significance of this rising tide of Yankeephobia lies in the fact that it choked the hemispheric spirit south of the Rio Grande. Other forms of association were sought; this was one reason for the popularity of the League of Nations in Latin America.[30] At one time or another, all of its twenty republics were members of the League.

Discontent boiled over at the Sixth Pan American Con-

[29] Luis-Alberto Sánchez, "A New Interpretation of the History of America," *Hispanic American Historical Review*, XXIII (1943), 444. See also Robert E. McNicoll, "Intellectual Origins of Aprismo," *ibid.*, 424–440.

[30] Warren H. Kelchner, *Latin American Relations with the League of Nations* (Boston, 1929), pp. 13–14.

ference, held at Havana in 1928.[31] The instructions to the United States delegates informed them that "among the Foreign Relations of the United States as they fall into categories, the Pan American policy takes first place in our diplomacy." [32] None but the United States' satellite states spoke of Hemisphere relations in like terms at Havana. Many of the delegates had come there determined to break the unwritten Pan American rule against the discussion of controversial questions and to pillory Uncle Sam. They did so. Intervention took first place in the wrangle, and Latin Americans were not appeased by chief delegate Charles Evans Hughes' assurance that the United States would never practice intervention but only "interposition." In the end, the best that could be obtained was an agreement to disagree and to discuss this and other matters on a later occasion. The economic policy of the United States also came in for sharp criticism, and when this was not answered to his satisfaction, the head of the influential Argentine delegation walked out of the meeting.

When the Conference adjourned, Pan Americanism was at ebb tide.[33] The authorities at Washington saw that the time had come when they would either have to change their ways radically or be left alone with their Hemisphere idea. Accordingly, in November President-elect Hoover set out on a South American good-will tour on a battleship; [34] and as soon as he took office in March 1929, the change began. Before the year was out, the first shock of the Great Depression had accelerated the rate of change. This change continued through the next two decades, but there was no continuity in the direction

[31] John P. Humphrey, *The Inter-American System: A Canadian View* (Toronto, 1942), pp. 92–93.

[32] Department of State, *Papers Relating to the Foreign Relations of the United States, 1928* (Washington, D.C., 1942), I, 534.

[33] Laurence Duggan, *The Americas: The Search for Hemisphere Security* (New York, 1949), p. 52.

[34] Alexander DeConde, *Herbert Hoover's Latin American Policy* (Stanford, 1951), p. 16.

of development. After 1930 Wilson's fellow countrymen duplicated his tergiversation regarding the Western Hemisphere idea by repeating, in the same order, first one and then the other of his two opposite excursions, so that while the 1930's saw the apotheosis of this idea, the 1940's witnessed its euthanasia.

VII ✒️

The Hemisphere of Peace

FROM the low-water mark reached at the time of the unhappy Havana Conference of 1928, Pan American sentiment
made a recovery which, though slow at first, carried it to
flood tide in the next decade. By 1940 the underlying Western
Hemisphere idea was more popular throughout the Americas
and apparently closer to realization than at any previous
period in its history.

One key to this success story is the development of the
United States' Good Neighbor Policy.[1] Unilateral in form but
multilateral in spirit, this policy was described in terms of
the French Revolutionary triad of liberty, equality, and fra-

[1] The most detailed study of this subject is Edward O. Guerrant, *Roosevelt's
Good Neighbor Policy* (Albuquerque, 1950), which is factual rather than
interpretative. The interested reader should also consult the relevant parts of
works of broader scope by Cordell Hull, *Memoirs* (2 vols., New York, 1948),
Sumner Welles, *The Time for Decision* (New York, 1944) and *Where Are We
Heading?* (New York, 1946), and Laurence Duggan, *The Americas* (New
York, 1949).

ternity.[2] It promised liberty to the Americas, in contrast to
the despotism being built up in Europe by Hitler and Mussolini and in Asia by Japan; equality in the sense of the juridical equality of all the American states, large and small; and
fraternity in the sense of a great increase in the degree and
range of co-operation and reciprocal assistance among the
American states. Though there were many exceptions, the
Latin Americans generally responded with enthusiasm.

There is also a second key to the success story: the identification of the Western Hemisphere as a haven of peace in a
war-tossed world. There was more than a suggestion of hemispheric isolationism in the reinvigorated American fellowship of this decade. As the reader will recall, there had also
been an isolationist seed in the Americanism of the early
nineteenth century, but now circumstances were even more
propitious to its growth. The original Western Hemisphere
idea of a peaceful, free America, united within itself and
separated from the broils of despot-ridden Europe, had never
seemed closer to realization, or, as many felt, more desirable,
than in the late 1930's. The climax came just after the fall of
France in 1940, when Canada and the orphaned European
colonies in America were apparently about to be drawn into
this fellowship, thus making Pan Americanism at last all-
American in fact as well as in name.

Credit Anstalt and Latin America

This upsurge was a far cry from the inauspicious beginning
of the decade on the morrow of the Havana Conference. At
first there was no promise of improvement, and in some ways
the situation even took a turn for the worse. In 1930 and 1931
a rash of "depression revolutions" broke out in Latin America;
even the larger and supposedly more stable countries such as

[2] In President Roosevelt's Pan American Day address, April 14, 1933, discussed below in the text and cited in note 18.

Argentina and Brazil suffered from them. Political gains
thought to have been securely made in the past half-century
of progress were wiped out in these revolutions, just as economic gains had been canceled by the depression that set
them off. Dictatorship took a new lease on life, economic
nationalism burgeoned, and the general atmosphere became
one of malaise and suspicion.

Much of the suspicion was directed against the United
States. As noted in the preceding essay, the latter had already
come to be regarded as a leading exponent of that capitalist-
imperialism which was held responsible for most of Latin
America's multiplying misfortunes, and now the wave of
revolts weakened its position still further in some parts of that
area. In Peru, for example, the pro-United States dictator
Augusto Leguía was overthrown, and the strongest party
that emerged under the new regime was Víctor Raúl Haya
de la Torre's violently Yankeephobe APRA. Again, in Brazil,
Getúlio Vargas, claiming that he had been counted out in a
presidential election, started a revolution; United States Secretary of State Henry L. Stimson prohibited the shipment of
arms from the United States to the revolutionists; Vargas
promptly won without them; and though Stimson had acted
in accordance with inter-American agreements and domestic
law, his action rankled with Brazil's new ruler.

During the four-year term of Stimson and his chief, President Hoover, from 1929 to 1933, the handling by the United
States of its Latin American affairs was legally correct, but
it did not win many friends. This is at first sight surprising,
because the Latin American policy of Hoover [3] and Stimson
was more than merely legally correct, and it was designed to
win friends by removing just causes for complaint on the part
of Latin Americans, particularly with reference to interven-

[3] For a well-documented and sympathetic account of this, see Alexander
DeConde, *Herbert Hoover's Latin-American Policy* (Stanford, 1949).

tion. A considerable measure of satisfaction was given them in both principle and practice; in principle, by jettisoning the Roosevelt corollary through the State Department's publication (in 1930) of the Clark Memorandum on the Monroe Doctrine; in practice, by beginning to reduce actual interventions. Likewise, Stimson abandoned Wilson's novel constitutional recognition policy, which was resented by Latin Americans as a form of diplomatic intervention, and returned to the classic, Jeffersonian policy of *de facto* recognition. In these and other ways, Hoover and Stimson did much to give the Latin American policy of the United States the benevolent character which it was to retain and develop in the administration of Franklin Roosevelt. In fact, the Good Neighbor Policy was born under Hoover, though it was baptised and came to maturity under Roosevelt.[4]

The trouble with the Hoover-Stimson policy was that it was largely negative. It remedied grievances by returning to the *status quo ante* Theodore Roosevelt and Wilson. It did not, however, provide leadership in blazing new trails in national or Pan American policy, nor did it encourage others to provide such leadership in the Pan American field. Its negative attitude was illustrated by its failure to take any kind of inter-American action to cope with the Great Depression, which afflicted all the American nations throughout all but

[4] I think this is a fair judgment on a highly controversial issue. Priority has been claimed for Hoover in the matter of the term "good neighbor" as well as the policy; e.g., DeConde, *op. cit.*, p. 18, cites Hoover's public use of it in 1928 on his preinauguration good-will tour of Latin America. But Hoover did not go on during his administration to get "good neighbor policy" and "Latin American policy" publicly recognized as virtually interchangeable terms, as Roosevelt was to do. Moreover, when Hoover used the term in 1928, "good neighbor" was already one of the most familiar clichés in the language of international intercourse. To give only one random illustration, President Mitre of Argentina used the term in precisely the same sense in his final address to the Argentine Congress in 1868: "Argentino ante todo, el Gobierno no dejará de ser americano y buen vecino" (Silva, *op. cit.*, p. 29). See further DeConde, *op. cit.*, pp. 126–127.

the first few months of Hoover's four-year administration.

As a champion of "rugged individualism," Hoover was opposed to government intervention in economic affairs, whether domestic or foreign, and the Western Hemisphere idea did not have a strong enough hold upon his administration to procure an exception to this general rule in the case of the Americas. That he had some sympathy for the Hemisphere idea when he came into office is indicated by his preinaugural good-will tour of Latin America mentioned at the close of the preceding chapter.[5] But his sympathy for it never carried him beyond the purpose of that trip, which was to stimulate general good will and the growth of inter-American trade through conventional private channels. When trade was, on the contrary, promptly prostrated by the depression, Hoover had no alternative to suggest. Indeed, he signed the Smoot-Hawley tariff act of 1930, which made matters even worse, and against which there had been strong Latin American protests during its passage through Congress.

For the most part, he left Latin American affairs to Secretary of State Stimson. Stimson was not primarily concerned with economic questions and was greatly relieved that the tariff did not fall within his jurisdiction. Moreover, his enthusiasm for the Western Hemisphere idea was conspicuous by its absence. If it had been otherwise, he might have been expected to take advantage of Canada's recent achievement of virtual independence to draw the northern neighbor into the Pan American family of nations. Instead, he left undisturbed the opposite policy, established in 1928 by the instructions to the American delegation to the Havana Conference: Canada, though now virtually independent, must not be admitted to the Pan American family, since its British Com-

[5] The tour began on November 10, 1928, lasted ten weeks, included four countries in Central America and six in South America (but not Mexico or Colombia), and was taken on the battleship *Maryland*. DeConde, *op. cit.*, p. 16.

monwealth ties kept it from being a truly American nation.[6]

Even in relation to Latin America, one needs a microscope to detect any trace of the Western Hemisphere idea either in Stimson's contemporaneous state papers and addresses or in his autobiography, *On Active Service in Peace and War* (1948). His attitude was rather like that of the Woodrow Wilson of the League of Nations period, from 1917 to 1921. Stimson was a globalist, not a regionalist, and he moved as far toward co-operation with the League as it was then politically feasible for a Washington policy maker to do.

It is true that, when he found it necessary for the United States to take action regarding intra-Latin American disputes, he insisted that it act on the basis of multilateral, inter-American co-operation, instead of unilaterally, as the preceding administration had done. Nevertheless, it seems clear that he did this in order to reduce the liabilities of the United States by sharing responsibility. His purpose was not to strengthen the inter-American system or to maintain, much less to promote, the Western Hemisphere idea.

He was already laying that stress upon the need for Anglo-American co-operation which was to play so decisive a part in his thinking about world affairs a few years later. While Stimson was Secretary of State, the British government was strongly opposed to the development of regionalism in any part of the world. The reasons for its opposition were clearly stated in a Foreign Office memorandum of 1930 on the French statesman Aristide Briand's plan for a European union. The memorandum condemned the proposal on the grounds that the formation of a European regional union would stimulate regional developments in Pan America and other parts of the

[6] On the 1928 instructions, see John P. Humphrey, "Canada," in Arthur P. Whitaker, ed., *Inter-American Affairs, 1942* (New York, 1943), pp. 44–45. On the general problem, see the same writer's *The Inter-American System: A Canadian View*, chs. i and ix. According to the index, DeConde, *op. cit.*, does not mention Canada.

world and that this would tend to break up the British Commonwealth and to weaken the League of Nations, support of which it described as "the sheet anchor of British foreign policy." [7] Whether or not Stimson was informed of the contents of this memorandum, he was well aware of the policy that inspired it, and this had his lively sympathy. He was no anticolonialist; and desiring a partnership with Britain, he wanted the British partner to be strong.

Moreover, when circumstances forced Stimson to think in regional terms, the areas to which he gave preferential attention were Europe and the Far East, not Latin America. His handling of relations with the latter gave the impression of a busy man getting necessary but minor matters cleared off his desk so that he might concentrate on the really important matters.

This attitude is faithfully reflected in Stimson's autobiography. Of the 130 pages which the book devotes to his work as Secretary of State, a scant fifteen pages, or one ninth of the whole, relate to Latin America.[8] Moreover, in his discussion of the Great Depression, as much space (half a page) is given to the collapse of one bank in Vienna, the Credit-Anstalt, as to the collapse of ten of the twenty Latin American governments; and while the Credit-Anstalt failure and its

[7] E. L. Woodward and Rohan Butler, eds., *Documents on British Foreign Policy, 1919–1939*, 2d ser., I (London, 1946), 331 (memorandum of May 30, 1930). A later memorandum (July 3, 1930) objected that the proposed European Federal Union "might—and probably would—give new strength both to the pan-American movement and to the Asiatic movement against Western domination" and that "these regionalising tendencies" might endanger both the "overriding authority" of the League of Nations and "the cohesion of the British Commonwealth of Nations" (*ibid.*, p. 341).

[8] Henry L. Stimson and McGeorge Bundy, *On Active Service in Peace and War* (New York, 1948), pp. 174–189. My statement in the text is not to be understood as reflecting on the general merits of this book, of which, in fact, I have a high opinion. This fact is evident in my article, "The Memoirs of Cordell Hull," *Hispanic American Historical Review*, XXIX (1949), 81–93, and my published lecture, "Three Autobiographies," *The Appel Memorial Lectures* (Lancaster, Pa., 1950), pp. 14–15.

aftermath are appropriately discussed in a chapter headed "The Beginnings of Disaster," the bankruptcy and revolutionizing of half Latin America receive their brief notice in the preceding chapter, which bears the caption "Constructive Beginnings."

This perspective and scale of values may be entirely right and proper, but that is not the question at issue. The important thing about it for our purpose is that it does not accord with the Western Hemisphere idea. The fact is worth noting, not only because Stimson's perspective and scale of values were shared by a good many of his fellow countrymen at that time but also because several years later (in 1940) he was to return again to high cabinet office and to aid greatly in establishing them in the nation's policy and public opinion and in its international commitments.[9]

"Modified isolationism"

It was in the interval between Stimson's two cabinet terms —from 1933 to 1940—that the Western Hemisphere idea enjoyed its heyday in the United States and America at large. His term in the State Department, along with that of Herbert Hoover in the White House, was brought to a close by the sweeping victory of the Democratic party, led by Franklin Roosevelt, in the national election of 1932.

Domestic issues, relating mainly to the depression, had dominated the electoral campaign. They also completely overshadowed foreign policy in the new President's inaugural address of March 4, 1933. Noticing the argument for international action in dealing with the depression only to brush it aside with the remark that first things must come first, Roosevelt devoted almost the whole of his address to the question of how to deal with the depression on the home front. Foreign policy he dismissed with a briefly pious dedication of

[9] See below, Essay VIII.

the United States to the "policy of the good neighbor" in its relations with all the rest of the world. This passage attracted little attention at the time for the very good reasons that there was nothing new about either the concept or even the term "good neighbor" [10] and that it was too vaguely stated here to have any definite meaning. Nor was there anything in the phraseology of this global statement of good neighborliness to enable one to foresee that it was soon to become exclusively identified with the policy of the United States toward Latin America.

Yet, in retrospect, the process of identification seems easy to trace. Some of the forces behind it were already at work. Japan was already on the march in Asia, and Hitler in Germany; Mussolini, emboldened by Hitler's rise, would soon be on the march in the Mediterranean; so that, shortly, Latin America was the only large group of nations in the world with which it was possible to maintain "good-neighborly" relations as defined by the United States.

The preceding administration's effort to improve hemispheric relations was continued and soon intensified. In the transition period early in 1933 Stimson's personal influence with Roosevelt and the incoming Secretary of State, Cordell Hull, may have helped to bring this about.[11] If so, Stimson's task must have been an easy one, for the kind of noninterventionist policy he had been following had been publicly advocated by Roosevelt as far back as 1928. In an article published that year in the well-known journal *Foreign Affairs,* Roosevelt had declared that the United States must abandon

[10] See above, note 4.

[11] Stimson and Bundy, *op. cit.,* pp. 288–296, "Middleman after Election" (i.e., middleman between the outgoing and incoming administrations), makes no specific reference to Latin America among the topics discussed by Stimson with Roosevelt and Hull, but it does state that these included "every major aspect of foreign policy" (p. 292) and "all the current problems of the State Department" (p. 294). It is to be hoped that the recently opened Stimson Papers (in the Yale University Library) will throw light on this question.

"for all time" the practice of "arbitrary interventions in the home affairs of our neighbors." [12] Moreover, one of Roosevelt's chief foreign policy advisers after 1933, Sumner Welles, first Assistant Secretary and then Under Secretary of State, had even earlier written a book on Santo Domingo with the Biblically allusive title of *Naboth's Vineyard,* in which he denied that there were hegemonic implications in the Monroe Doctrine and called for the development of more active Pan American co-operation on the basis of the equality of all the American states.[13]

We must also take note of the existence during Roosevelt's first administration of a fundamental national attitude which, while not specifically related to Latin American policy, was nevertheless an essential condition of its development. This was the resurgence of isolationism, both implicitly in the administration and most explicitly in the country at large. The attitude of Roosevelt's first administration in this matter has been generally forgotten because of his later leadership of internationalism, but it is the considered opinion of a leading authority on the history of United States foreign policy in this period that "viewed in the context of the early years of the Roosevelt Administration, even the Good Neighbor Policy was only an expression of a modified isolationism." [14] Whipped up by so-called revelations of how during World War I the United States had been deceived and exploited by wicked European statesmen and selfish American bankers and merchants of death, public opinion went much further in demanding, and from 1935 to 1937 obtaining, neutrality legislation which sacrificed vital features of the coun-

[12] Franklin D. Roosevelt, "Our Foreign Policy," *Foreign Affairs,* VI (1928), 573–586.

[13] Sumner Welles, *Naboth's Vineyard: The Dominican Republic, 1844–1924* (New York, 1928), II, 918–925.

[14] William L. Langer, "Political Problems of a Coalition," *Foreign Affairs,* XXVI (1947), 75.

try's traditional neutrality policy in the hope of insulating it against another "foreign" war.

But the isolationist temper of the public at large was never more strikingly expressed than in the spontaneous and nation-wide protest that greeted Roosevelt's first open indication that he himself was beginning to shift from his original "modified isolationism" to a mildly internationalist position. This indication was given, shortly after the beginning of his second term, in his now famous "Quarantine Address," delivered at Chicago in October 1937, in which he proposed that the peace-loving nations quarantine the aggressor nations. So massive and violent was the protest that Roosevelt beat a hasty retreat and did not return openly to the charge until the winter of 1940, when he proposed Lend-Lease to make the United States the "arsenal of democracy."

Finally, both before and during Roosevelt's administration, the Western Hemisphere idea enjoyed an increasing vogue in certain intellectual circles in the United States. Many examples could be given from the works of Charles A. Beard and other members of the intelligentsia, and some of these will be mentioned later in another connection. But the one chosen for discussion here is a particularly striking example because it is provided by an address designed for a professional group who presumably averaged higher in intellectual standards and lower in emotional voltage than the general public. This was the presidential address delivered by the late Herbert Eugene Bolton, as president of the American Historical Association, at its meeting in Toronto, Canada, in December 1932. The title he gave it was "The Epic of Greater America," [15] meaning by "Greater America" the whole Western Hemisphere. A twofold theme runs through the address: first, the unity of the history of the

[15] Herbert E. Bolton, *Wider Horizons of American History* (New York, 1939), pp. 1–54, "The Epic of Greater America."

Western Hemisphere peoples; and second, their growing solidarity.

In developing these themes, Bolton recapitulated expressions of the Western Hemisphere idea dating back to the early nineteenth century. Three examples must suffice. These are, first, the intermingling of the mystical with the rational; second, the political application of the Hemisphere idea; and third, the antithesis of America versus Europe.

As for the mingling of mystical and rational, much of what Bolton said would pass muster in the most hard-headed group of historians, yet along with this he occasionally (and at critical points) exhibited the faith that moves mountains— of historical evidence. Nowhere did he exhibit it more clearly than in the assertion that "the essential unity of the Western Hemisphere was revealed by [the First World War]. . . . There was emphatic Western Hemisphere solidarity [during that war]." [16] This must have been faith at work, for it was not history.

Bolton's political application of the Western Hemisphere idea is illustrated by the following passage in his address:

The increasing importance of inter-American relations makes imperative a better understanding by each of the history and culture of all. A synthetic view is important not alone for its present-day political and commercial implications; it is quite as desirable from the standpoint of correct historiography.

and again

Ever since independence there has been fundamental Western Hemisphere solidarity.

This is immediately followed by a passage which illustrates the Europe versus America antithesis:

Therefore, it is not a matter of indifference [warned Bolton] to know that European influence in South America today far out-

[16] *Ibid.*, p. 49.

143

weighs that of Saxon America, and that Europe is bending every effort to draw the Southern continent more and more into the European circle and away from its northern neighbors.[17]

The burgeoning Americanism of Bolton's generation which is illustrated by this address also had its counterpart in the Latin America of that period. There it had a rather explosive character, and perhaps what touched it off was the series of centennial celebrations of independence which were held in many of the Latin American countries in or shortly after 1910. To be sure, the Americanism thus expressed was seldom continental; frequently it was nothing more than a narrow nationalism. But all the expressions of it did at least have America as their common theme, and the problem (already noted in another connection in an earlier essay) was so to develop this theme as to synthesize all these little Americas in one Pan America—or, as Bolton called it, Greater America. This, for a brief moment of history, the Good Neighbor Policy succeeded largely in accomplishing.

Good Neighbors

For several months after Roosevelt's inaugural address of March 4, 1933, little or nothing was done toward whittling down the good-neighbor concept from global to hemispheric proportions. Six weeks later, on Pan American Day, Roosevelt delivered a ceremonial address which poured the irenic phraseology of March 4 into a Pan American mold, but there was still no suggestion that it could not just as well be poured into some other mold on a similar festive occasion. And, as Samuel F. Bemis has pointed out, the address "did not announce any new policy." For us, its interest lies mainly in the fact that in this, his first formal pronouncement of his Latin American policy, Roosevelt stated that policy in terms of the French Revolutionary triad with almost crystal clarity—"al-

[17] *Ibid.*, pp. 2, 50.

most," because the term liberty was only implied. It was, however, clearly implied in the President's reference to "the maintenance of independence by the peoples of the [American] continent," particularly the maintenance of their independence against aggression "in this hemisphere by any non-American power." The other two terms were stated explicitly: "Your Americanism and mine," he went on, "must be a structure built of confidence, cemented by sympathy, which recognizes only equality and fraternity." [18]

The identification of the good neighbor with the Latin American neighbor began after the fiasco of the London World Economic Conference in July of that same year, which followed hard on the heels of the petering out of the Geneva Conference on the limitation of armaments; and there are reasons for believing that the identification was greatly facilitated by these two failures. One reason for thinking so is provided by Secretary of State Cordell Hull's explanation of his insistence upon going through with the Inter-American Conference scheduled to be held at Montevideo in December 1933. From Argentina and other quarters, strong pressure was put upon him to agree to a postponement,[19] but he was adamant in his refusal—not because he had any particular program in mind, for his memoirs make it clear that he had none until one was thought up on the 6,000-mile sea voyage from New York to Montevideo,[20] but because, as he tells us, he wanted to offset the European failures at London and Geneva with an inter-American success at Montevideo.[21]

The Montevideo Conference was held as scheduled, and it was a tremendous success, at least in generating hemispheric good will. This was accomplished mainly through judicious horse trading on the part of Secretary Hull, the details of which cannot be described here, except to note the chief

[18] Quoted in Bemis, *Latin American Policy*, p. 430, n. 6.
[19] Hull, *op. cit.*, I, 317.   [20] *Ibid.*, I, 319.   [21] *Ibid.*, I, 317–320.

concession made by the United States, which was its acceptance, subject to a little-noticed reservation, of a ban on
intervention. The Conference thereupon turned into a love
feast. The contrast with the suspicion and bitterness of the
preceding Havana Conference of 1928 could hardly have
been more complete. At Havana, the chief Argentine delegate
had left the Conference after a disagreement with the United
States. At Montevideo, the world was treated to the almost
unbelievable spectacle of the Argentine Foreign Minister,
Carlos Saavedra Lamas, playing Damon to the Pythias of
the United States Secretary of State, Cordell Hull.

Montevideo promoted the Americanization of the originally
global Good Neighbor Policy. It also ushered in the heyday
of the new Pan Americanism. With Secretary Hull, the heady
wine of success at Montevideo was an incitement to more
good works in the same spirit; Welles, like-minded, carried
most of the burden; and Roosevelt, absorbed in the perplexing
domestic problems of the New Deal, gave these two their
head. The rest of the intervention structure was soon dis-
mantled. The thirty-year-old Platt Amendment (which had
been its cornerstone) was scrapped by a new treaty with
Cuba in 1934, and a similar change was made in the case of
Panama by the treaty of 1936 (though ratification of this was
held up, for defense reasons, until early 1939). The culminat-
ing step was taken in 1936 at the Buenos Aires Inter-American
Conference on Peace and Security: there the United States
agreed to an absolute ban on all intervention, this time without reservation.

This was all very well, and it fanned the fire of enthusiasm
for the Hemisphere idea in both Americas; but it was, after
all, only a completion of what Hoover and Stimson had begun;
and even when brought to complete success, that remained a
negative policy. If the Hemisphere idea was to thrive, a
positive content must be poured into it, and there still re-

mained the uncomfortable paradox that Pan Americanism, though based upon the Hemisphere idea, embraced much less than the whole Hemisphere so long as Canada remained outside.

The new Pan Americanism

In both respects great advances were made, mainly under the aegis of the Good Neighbor Policy, before the decade was over. In the former respect, they were in fact well begun by the time the process of remedying Latin American grievances had been completed at Buenos Aires in 1936. The new positive content was both economic and military. The economic theme was introduced at the Montevideo Conference of 1933, thanks to the initiative of Cordell Hull, but there it produced only a statement of principles, aimed mainly at lowering barriers to international trade. The more practical expression of the economic theme began in 1934 on a very small scale and as an outgrowth of the national policy of the United States in the use of funds of a United States government agency, the Export-Import Bank, to ease the difficult economic situation in Cuba.[22] From this modest beginning, inter-American economic co-operation spread rapidly in the next few years.[23] To co-ordinate and extend effort in this field, an Inter-American Financial and Economic Advisory Committee was set up when war broke out in Europe in 1939, and the new committee in turn produced inter-American offshoots such as a coffee agreement and development commissions.

These efforts were necessarily supported mainly by the United States, and frequently they were carried out on a bilateral basis; but more and more they took on the cast of Hemisphere co-operation. Indeed, they showed strong signs of developing into a system of Hemisphere self-sufficiency, somewhat along the lines advocated by several influential

[22] *Ibid.,* I, 344.   [23] Duggan, *op. cit.,* pp. 78–82.

writers, among them Charles A. Beard and Stuart Chase. Two of Beard's books, *The Open Door at Home* (1934) and *A Foreign Policy for the United States* (1939), gave the Hemisphere approach its best literary expression.

In the field of public policy, this approach was best expressed in the Hemisphere cartel plan proposed in 1940 to meet the dire emergency created by the fall of France. Drafted by Nelson Rockefeller and publicly announced by President Roosevelt on June 21, 1940,[24] the cartel plan was in fact the most extreme economic expression ever given the Western Hemisphere idea. The starting point of the plan was the creation of an inter-American trading corporation for the purchase and disposal of surplus commodities. But it went far beyond this, for it proposed among other things the reduction or elimination of tariffs, together with the following recommendations:

Compensation to United States industrial and agricultural interests unfavorably affected; private and government investment in Latin America for development of raw material resources; expansion of government services . . . development of cultural, scientific and educational relationships.

In addition, production was to be reorganized on a long-term basis. In presenting the plan, Rockefeller announced the Western Hemisphere theme in no uncertain terms. He said in the introduction:

If the United States is to maintain its security and its political and economic hemisphere position, it must take economic measures at once to secure economic prosperity in Central and South America; and to establish this prosperity in the frame of hemisphere economic cooperation and dependence.

[24] William L. Langer and S. Everett Gleason, *The Challenge to Isolation, 1937–1940* (New York, 1952), pp. 631–635.

"For reasons that are still obscure," we are told in a recent and highly authoritative work,[25] the cartel plan was abruptly abandoned. This was perhaps because of the unfavorable popular reaction to it but more probably because of the opposition of Secretary Hull, who disliked its New-Deal, government-intervention flavor and preferred his own well-established trade agreements program. In any case, on sober second thought, American policy makers realized that the Hemisphere frame of the cartel plan was not large enough, that the Western Hemisphere was not, and could not in the foreseeable future become, a viable economic unit.

Similarly, in the field of military security the Americas rapidly developed a co-operative system. Here, too, there was for a brief moment a strong tendency toward isolationism; once again the tendency was arrested by the second-look realization that the Western Hemisphere could not live apart from the rest of the world, but must somehow contrive to come to terms with it. So widespread and deeply rooted was the Hemisphere sentiment which stimulated this tendency that the first formalization of continental security (which was accomplished in 1936 by the so-called Pan Americanization of the Monroe Doctrine at the Buenos Aires Conference) was followed within three years by a close approach to Hemisphere isolationism.

The approach was made at the Panama meeting of American Foreign Ministers in 1939, just after the outbreak of war in Europe.[26] Verbally, the meeting at Panama disclaimed isolationist thoughts, but its most striking action told another tale. This was the three-hundred-mile-wide neutrality zone which, without regard for international law, the delegates

[25] *Ibid.*, p. 634.

[26] There is a good account of this meeting in Whitney H. Shepardson and William O. Scroggs, *The United States in World Affairs, 1939* (New York, 1940), pp. 194–211.

undertook to spread out over the high seas bordering on the American republics. Scoffers called it the Pan American chastity belt.

No doubt the delegates' disclaimers of Hemisphere isolationism were sincere, but inter-American policy was tending in that direction. The prevalent view seemed to be that even if isolationism was not a policy that the Americas ought deliberately to adopt, it was a condition which the state of the world was thrusting upon them, and they must make the best of it. The United States delegate, Sumner Welles, who was certainly no isolationist, cited in defense of the neutrality zone the

right inherent in their [the twenty-one American republics'] position as peaceful and independent powers, constituting an entire continent . . . to protect themselves . . . from . . . the repercussions of a war which has broken out thousands of miles from their shores and in which they are not involved.

And he continued:

We have created an American system, an American way of life, which is our chief contribution to world civilization. . . . As the shadows created by the outbreak of this monstrous war darken and spread rapidly across the length and breadth of the world . . . the twenty-one free nations of the New World can still preserve for posterity those ideals and those beliefs which may well constitute the last great hope of the civilization which we have inherited.[27]

Canada and the colonies

By 1943 Welles's twenty-one free New World nations of 1939 had become, in a speech which he delivered at Toronto, Canada, "twenty-two independent democracies." [28] The new-

[27] Sumner Welles, *The World of the Four Freedoms* (New York, 1943), pp. 9–10.
[28] *Ibid.*, p. 120.

comer was, of course, his host country, Canada. The change is an indication of what then seemed a trend toward making the Pan American system actually all-American and thus bringing the Western Hemisphere idea to full fruition. According to Canadian writers, Canada had long been the linchpin between Britain and the United States; it had certainly had very strong ties with both. In the late 1930's and early 40's its ties with the United States and, through it, with the Western Hemisphere, were further strengthened. A notable example was the Hyde Park Declaration of April 1941, which was made in the name of Hemisphere defense as well as local defense.[29] At the other end, however, the Canadian linchpin was in danger of being snapped by the fall of Britain—or at least, so it seemed on the western side of the Atlantic, where a German invasion of Britain was regarded as imminent in the latter half of 1940 and as by no means unthinkable in the next two years.

In these years there was a vigorous revival of talk about the incorporation of Canada into the Pan American system. This possibility had long been considered, and in the Pan American Union building in Washington, one of the twenty-two chairs initially provided for the use of the Union's Governing Board bore the arms of Canada, which were also displayed on the walls along with the emblems of the other American states.[30] Hitherto the prospect of Canada's accession had seemed remote, but in 1942 a Canadian writer, John P. Humphrey, declared not only that it was his country's "obvious international duty" to "join the Union of American states" but that "Canada cannot afford to remain outside the rapidly developing system of hemisphere defence." [31] Without specific reference to Pan Americanism, his compatriot

[29] Bartlett, op. cit., p. 561.
[30] Humphrey, The Inter-American System, p. 202.
[31] Ibid., p. 261.

F. R. Scott had already noted that the Ogdensburg Agreement of 1940 with the United States was the first defense commitment Canada had ever made with a country outside the British Commonwealth, and he asked, "Is Canada moving into the American orbit?" [32]

There were also signs in these years that the Americanization of the last remaining European possessions in the New World was at hand. The European powers that owned them were France, the Netherlands, and Britain. When in May and June 1940 Hitler's troops overran the first two countries and then poised themselves to pounce on the third, the American republics promptly prepared to take over the "orphaned" American colonies of the three victims and govern them under inter-American auspices, rather than let them fall into Hitler's hands. For reasons of his own, Hitler chose not to force the issue, with the result that the orphanage plan was never carried out. Yet even so there was a widespread feeling that the time had come when the long process of the emancipation of America from European tutelage should, and somehow or other would, be completed. The first stages of the process—the establishment of the independence of the United States and Latin America—had led to the formulation of the Western Hemisphere idea and its political application; the last stage would bring it to fulfillment.

Doubting Thomases might—and did—raise questions about the isolationist connotations of the idea, or about its value, whether isolationist or not, under mid-twentieth-century conditions of power politics. But, as of 1940, it had in its favor the overwhelming argument of success. In the past ten years it had been applied on an unprecedented and ever-increasing scale. It was acclaimed in Latin America, and even more warmly in the United States, where statesmen, soldiers, businessmen, journalists, and clubwomen delighted to honor

[32] F. R. Scott, *Canada and the United States* (Boston, 1941), p. 7.

it, and where the nation's three foreign policy makers, Roosevelt, Hull, and Welles, raised paeans in praise of Pan Americanism. In short, as the decade of the 40's opened, political astronomers could well believe that the Western Hemisphere idea was still in the ascendant.

VIII ⚘

Two Worlds, New Style:

Reunion with Europe

THE present essay deals with the latest phase of the long history of the Western Hemisphere idea, from 1940 to the present. The indications are that it will also prove the last phase, in the sense in which we have defined the idea in these pages. This fact has been obscured by the extension that has been given to the forms of inter-American co-operation since 1940, but one must distinguish between form and substance. After 1940 the substance of the Western Hemisphere idea was lost, and its place was taken first and briefly by globalism and then by new twofold divisions of the globe, not into the traditional Eastern and Western hemispheres, but into

154

Northern and Southern hemispheres, or, more frequently, into the communist and noncommunist worlds. Both of these new-style divisions of the world grouped Western Europe with all or most of America, and thus they were in headlong conflict with the classic Western Hemisphere idea, an essential component of which was the separation of America from Europe.

In describing this process we shall have to deal mainly with the United States, which is hardly surprising since the Western Hemisphere idea owed its origin and growth largely to this country. The story we are about to tell stands in such sharp contrast to that of the preceding decade, to which the term flood tide was applied, that one is tempted to preserve the metaphor and speak of the tide as ebbing sharply in this latest phase. But the metaphor will no longer serve, since to all appearances the tide has gone out never to return, which means that it is no proper tide. A better figure would be euthanasia, for the end of the Western Hemisphere idea came so peacefully that it has passed almost unnoticed down to the present time.

Still better is the analogy of a glacier. A British authority on that interesting phenomenon of inanimate nature, Dr. C. E. P. Brooks, tells us that because "the snow which falls on a mountain peak may not melt at the glacier's end until a century later . . . [and] the size of a glacier averages the weather," hence "a few of the longest glaciers . . . are still advancing while most are in full retreat." [1] The Pan American movement is one of the long glaciers of modern history. Its recent advances represent Hemisphere snow that fell as much as fifty or a hundred years ago. Now the international climate that produced it has changed. How long will it be before it is in full retreat?

[1] C. E. P. Brooks, "What Is Happening to the Weather?" *Harper's Magazine,* January 1953, pp. 35–36.

Revolt against the "Western Hemisphere complex"

The fall of France in 1940 and Britain's refusal to fall gave a decisive stimulus to a gathering revolt in the United States against the Western Hemisphere idea, which many had come to regard as a false façade for isolationism. Though there had been sporadic resistance to it even earlier, the revolt against the idea became widespread only when President Roosevelt sparked it by his Quarantine Address of October 1937. He probably did so unintentionally, for his shaft was directed against isolationism, not Pan Americanism, to which he had given and still gave warm support. Many other anti-isolationists, however, made no such distinction, but on the contrary regarded Pan Americanism as a stalking-horse for isolationists. There was some justification for this view; as the following pages will show, the identification of the two with each other became so close in the next few years that the ultimate defeat of isolationism contributed greatly to the decline of the Western Hemisphere idea.

In 1937, however, the isolationists were still riding high, and they raised so great a clamor against the Quarantine Address that the President, fearing political disaster, retreated into silence.[2] So did his political lieutenants, but not the interventionists in private life. The latter kept up the fight; and while at that time they neither had a national organization nor were in common agreement upon a specific goal, nevertheless they developed something like a concerted movement in favor of some kind of active resistance to tyranny and aggression in Europe and Asia.

Their first two years of effort brought about little change in public opinion and none in public policy. The outbreak of

[2] Langer and Gleason, *op. cit.*, pp. 11, 18–19. By January 1938 Roosevelt had swung so far the other way that he had adopted a project which "though involving no approval of British appeasement . . . certainly implied acceptance of it" (*ibid.*, p. 25).

war in Europe in September 1939 got their third year off to an even more discouraging start. At the moment, hatred of war was even greater than hatred of Hitler in the United States.[3]

Hatred of war found positive expression in devotion to the Western Hemisphere idea. No phrase was more popular at that time than "the hemisphere of peace." As we have more than once seen, the proposition implicit in this phrase—that America must cut itself off from the perpetual broils of Europe —was one of the oldest and most potent ingredients of the larger Western Hemisphere idea. Sanctified by long tradition, it had by 1940 acquired almost the force of scriptural injunction. As many, perhaps most, Americans still read their history at that time, the violation of this injunction in 1917 had had its due punishment in the lost peace of 1919. Instinctive loyalty to the traditional faith was strong throughout the Americas, and certainly not least so in the United States.

At first in 1940, even the shock of Hitler's quite unexpected conquests from Norway to France produced in most Americans the motor response of "continentalism and more continentalism"—as in the Hemisphere cartel plan drawn up in June 1940 and discussed in the preceding essay. That is hardly surprising when one recalls that continentalism was the response which for more than a century past the Western Hemisphere idea had conditioned the American people to give. But when the initial shock wore off, many of them took another look and decided that to stop with this motor response would be suicidal; and so they re-examined the ideological basis of the conditioning that had produced it. They soon came up with the answer: the Western Hemisphere idea was only a myth, and since it had become a dangerous myth, it could not be too soon abandoned.

The lead in discovering and advertising this answer was
[3] *Ibid.,* pp. 12–14.

taken by the already mobilized interventionists. Their effectiveness was greatly increased because they now had a specific goal (all-out-aid to beleaguered Britain) and a national organization (William Allen White's Committee to Defend America by Aiding the Allies).[4] One member of this group was the then little-known Dean Acheson, who was one of the four New York lawyers who in the summer of 1940 helped to find a satisfactory solution for the difficult legal and diplomatic problem of the destroyer-bases deal with Great Britain.[5]

The climax of the great debate between isolationists and interventionists came in the year and a half between the fall of France and the Japanese attack on Pearl Harbor; it was also a debate between continentalists and globalists. We cannot follow it better at the policy-making level than by looking at it from the point of view of the most eminent of the interventionists, Henry L. Stimson. This was the same Stimson who, as President Hoover's Secretary of State, had helped to lay the foundations of the Good Neighbor Policy, but he had done so without the faintest notion that it would develop into a Pan Americanism strongly tinged with Hemisphere isolationism. In July 1940 he became Secretary of War in President Roosevelt's cabinet, and he made the most of the prime opportunity that this position afforded him to correct that grievous error, as he judged it to be. But he realized that the heresy had great popular support, and, prudent strategist that he was, he moved against it not in a headlong frontal attack but by a flanking movement.

How prudent this course was is suggested by the results of a Gallup Poll taken in April 1941. This showed that even at that late date four fifths of the American people were still

[4] *Ibid.*, pp. 486–487, 505–507, 710–711; Walter Johnson, *The Battle against Isolation* (Chicago, 1944), ch. iii, "The Internationalists Organize."

[5] Langer and Gleason, *op. cit.*, pp. 711, 757.

opposed to immediate entry into the war, although in the same ratio they thought the United States would enter it sooner or later, and three fourths of them were in favor of entering it "if it appeared certain that there was no other way to defeat Germany and Italy." [6]

Statesmen must take account of this state of mind and feeling, and, however reluctantly, Stimson did so. When in July 1940 he appeared before the Senate committee that was to pass upon the confirmation of his appointment as Secretary of War, he invoked the Monroe Doctrine itself in defense of his advocacy of aid to Britain. To continentalists, this was like the devil quoting scripture. Under modern conditions of warfare, he declared, the Monroe Doctrine could be enforced only by extending the American line of defense "far out into the Atlantic Ocean." [7] Even Stimson at this time did not admit that he was really proposing to extend the line of defense all the way across the Atlantic Ocean, so that what his proposition amounted to was that under modern conditions the Monroe Doctrine could be enforced only by violating its basic principle, the injunction against involvement in the broils of Europe—in other words, that it could not be maintained at all.

President Roosevelt was even more wary of offending the myriad devotees of the Hemisphere tradition. He inched ahead along the line desired by Stimson, but so very slowly and under cover of so thick a smoke screen of continentalism as to cause intense irritation to his more forthright Secretary of War.

Thus, according to Roosevelt, all that he did was designed to keep war away from America, to preserve the Hemisphere of peace. It was in this guise that he presented to Congress and the nation his crucially important proposal of January 1941 for making the United States the "arsenal of democracy"

[6] Stimson and Bundy, *op. cit.*, p. 374.   [7] *Ibid.*, pp. 325–326.

through Lend-Lease. Stimson applauded the measure enthusiastically as "a declaration of economic war"; [8] but in the following months he was deeply disappointed by the President's failure to provide the country with energetic leadership in pursuing the line thus indicated and breaking the last shackles of neutrality and the Hemisphere tradition.[9]

Disagreement between the two on this point was sharp in the matter of the United States' military occupation of Iceland. In July 1941 Roosevelt decided to inform Congress and the public that the occupation had taken place. The question arose as to the terms in which this extraordinary if not quite unprecedented measure should be publicly explained. Stimson argued for a frank admission of the true reason, which was that it was essential to the protection of the North Atlantic sea route over which munitions and other war supplies were being sent from America to Britain. Roosevelt, however, decided to "build his case mainly on the defense of the Western Hemisphere." He did so because he believed this would make it "more palatable . . . to the people" and "less subject to violent attack from the isolationists." His decision pained Stimson, who complained that on this occasion as on others in this transition period, "the chance for a trumpet call for a battle to save freedom throughout the world had been sunk in a quibble over the extent of defense and the limits of the Western Hemisphere." [10]

Some leaders of the revolt

The views cautiously advocated by Stimson were publicized at this time by writers who, not being active in political

---

[8] *Ibid.*, p. 360. [9] *Ibid.*, pp. 366–376.

[10] *Ibid.*, p. 373. Basil Rauch, *Roosevelt from Munich to Pearl Harbor* (New York, 1950), pp. 194–196, tells how, although Roosevelt treated Greenland as a part of the Western Hemisphere, he rejected the State Department's view that Iceland too was "largely" a part of it "because the strain on the public idea of geography would be too severe."

life, could speak out more boldly. Their writings reflected the sweeping change of ideas then in progress regarding the role of the United States in world affairs. The change was due in part to the influence of a British writer, Sir Halford Mackinder, and the German school of geopolitics, founded by General Haushofer. They taught many Americans for the first time to think globally and in terms of power politics.

One of the most important results was that Americans learned to look at the map in a new way. That is important because the Western Hemisphere idea owed its origin partly to a particular view of the map—the view suggested by the conventional eighteenth- and nineteenth-century maps which divided the globe neatly and definitively into flat hemispheres, Eastern and Western, and gave the Americas an appearance of continental unity. But times had changed, and with them the way of making maps. As Mackinder said, "The geographical perspective of the twentieth century differs . . . from that of all previous centuries." [11] The geographical perspective which he then proceeded to offer his readers made this seem a masterpiece of understatement, at least from the American point of view. He placed the "heartland" of the world in Europe-Asia and pictured the land areas of the world as consisting of "the World Island and its satellites," with Europe-Asia-Africa as the World Island and with North and South America not merely reduced to satellite status but divided into two separate satellite islands.[12]

A prime example of the application of the new ideas to the current controversy between isolationists and interventionists is the slashing attack on the Western Hemisphere idea made by Eugene Staley in an article entitled "The Myth of the Continents," published in April 1941.[13] It appeared in the

[11] Halford J. Mackinder, *Democratic Ideals and Reality* (New York, 1942), p. 29. This book was first published in 1919.

[12] *Ibid.*, p. 67.

[13] Eugene Staley, "The Myth of the Continents," *Foreign Affairs*, XIX

quarterly journal *Foreign Affairs,* which reached a restricted
but very influential group of readers. Within the larger framework indicated by its title, this article was primarily an attack on what its author called "the Western Hemisphere complex."[14] He began with a notice of three recent popular books,
all by well-known writers—Charles A. Beard, Jerome Frank,
and Stuart Chase [15]—all of which were dominated by this
complex; they abounded in such terms as "continentalism,"
"relative self-sufficiency," and "integrated America," which
they contrasted with "disintegrated Europe." Staley then proceeded to demolish these isolationists' fundamental premise
by demonstrating the general proposition that continental
unity is a myth, and that oftener than not, land divides while
water unites.

In the particular case of the American continent, he pointed
out how the northern and southern halves of it are in fact
united only by sea or air and how greater distances (whether
by land, sea, or air) separate the United States from important points in America than from other points in Europe,
Africa, and Asia. For example, puckishly taking as his point

(1941), 481–494. The editor gave it the place of honor as the leading article
in this issue. A similarly telling argument from the economic point of view was
presented by Percy W. Bidwell, *Economic Defense of Latin America* (Boston,
1941), ch. v, "The Fallacy of Hemisphere Self-Sufficiency."

[14] Staley, *op. cit.,* p. 481: "The Western Hemisphere complex, so conspicuous in discussions of American foreign policy, has often been associated
with ideas of 'continental' unity and 'continental' solidarity." For quite dif-
ferent reasons, the "Western Hemisphere complex" as expressed in the new
Pan Americanism also came under heavy fire from some quarters in Latin
America during this critical period, mainly on the ground that the United
States was strengthening the American regional system for its own fell pur-
poses, which were not sufficiently isolationist to suit the Latin American critics.
A good example is Felipe Barreda Laos, *Hispano América en guerra?* (Buenos
Aires, 1941); the author was the Ambassador of Peru to Argentina and
Uruguay at that time.

[15] The books cited were Beard's *A Foreign Policy for the United States*
(New York, 1940), Frank's *Save America First* (New York, 1938), and
Chase's *The New Western Front* (New York, 1939). See Staley, *op. cit.,* p.
481.

of reference in the United States Madison, Wisconsin, the home town of a leading isolationist, Governor LaFollette, he noted that "no capital in Europe, including Moscow, is as far from Madison as is Buenos Aires, and only one European capital (Athens) is as far as Rio de Janeiro. . . . This is direct-line distance, and by actually travelled routes Europe is relatively closer." [16] By these and other arguments which we cannot go into here, he reached the following conclusion:

The United States should regard western hemisphere defense lines as distinctly secondary, to be prepared for emergency use if the first line breaks . . . It is less risky to stand now for all-out defense, together with Britain, of the seas and the strong-points commanding the seas of the whole world . . . than to let Britain go down and then try to defend the western hemisphere practically alone. [17]

Some of the principal points in this article were by no means new. Far back in the nineteenth century, the Argentine writer Juan Bautista Alberdi, discussing the same question, had pointed out that the seas do not divide but unite and that the modern revolution in the means of transportation and communications had already begun to merge the peoples of all lands in a single world society (*pueblo-mundo*).[18] Again, in an article published in 1927 in this same journal, *Foreign Affairs,* Archibald Cary Coolidge had anticipated Staley in calling attention to obvious flaws in the assumptions underlying Pan Americanism.[19] But Coolidge, in the relative calm and security of 1927, noted without concern that Pan Americanism rested on faith, not fact. Staley, in the tempest of 1941, used the same discrepancy between fact and faith to prove that the country must rid itself at once of its "western hemisphere complex."

[16] Pages 485–486.   [17] Page 494.   [18] See above, Essay IV.
[19] Archibald Cary Coolidge, "The Grouping of Nations," *op. cit.,* pp. 182–183. Coolidge was probably best known for his book, *The United States as a World Power,* dealing mainly with the decade after 1898.

His article now has the air of an *ad hoc* argument for aid to Britain, but it was much more than that. It marked a turning point—a downward-turning point—in the history of the Western Hemisphere idea. The editor of *Foreign Affairs* was eminently justified in including it in *The Foreign Affairs Reader*,[20] a twenty-fifth anniversary volume published in 1947, containing about thirty articles culled from among more than a thousand articles published in that journal in the past quarter-century and "selected," explained the editor, "because what their authors had to say seems a permanent part of the record." This article, be it noted, is the only one in the volume which deals with Latin America or Pan America. At any time before 1941 such a proportion would have been unthinkable; since 1941 it has been about right.

Another heavy blow to the traditional Western Hemisphere faith was delivered in 1942 by a work of hard-boiled realism, Nicholas J. Spykman's *America's Strategy in World Politics*. Its author described it as a new approach in geopolitical terms to "the most basic issue of American foreign policy," that of isolation versus intervention, in an effort to "develop a grand strategy for both war and peace based on the implications of [the United States'] geographic location in the world." [21]

Spykman's book is therefore one of prime importance for our purpose, since hitherto the geographic location of the United States in the world had served as one of the chief supports of the Western Hemisphere idea and Pan Americanism. He gave these much attention and short shrift. His case against them was based not only on geographical considerations such as those advanced by Mackinder, Haushofer, and Staley but also on the weakness of the Latin American states. "Because the Latin American states are weak," he wrote,

[20] Hamilton Fish Armstrong, ed., *The Foreign Affairs Reader* (New York, 1947), pp. 318–333.

[21] Nicholas John Spykman, *America's Strategy in World Politics* (New York, 1942), p. 7.

"they cannot threaten the security of the northern republic and because of that fact, their relations to Washington can never be as important as those of the great powers of Europe and Asia." [22] This turned upside down the proposition set forth in the State Department's instructions of 1928 to the delegates to the Pan American Conference at Havana: "It is an established principle of our international policy that: 'Among the Foreign Relations of the United States as they fall into categories, the Pan American policy takes first place in our diplomacy.'"

Spykman also judged Pan Americanism by its works and found it wanting. [23] But perhaps his most telling blow was struck by his identification of Pan Americanism with isolationism. Briefly sketching the historical process by which this identification had come about, he wrote:

The size of the geographic area in the New World necessary for the creation of an adequate system of defense gradually expanded in the minds of the isolationists [in the United States]. Originally it was the national domain; after the building of the Panama Canal it was extended to include the Caribbean littoral and finally the whole hemisphere. . . . Hemisphere defense through hemisphere isolation became the new streamlined version of the old isolationist position. [24]

This was in some respects not good history, but it was extremely effective propaganda against Pan Americanism and "the western hemisphere complex." Its timing was perfect, for it pinned the isolationist stigma on Pan Americanism at the very moment when isolationism became a lost cause. Just before Spykman's book was published, the isolationists in the United States were routed by the Japanese attack on

[22] *Ibid.*, pp. 352–353.
[23] *Ibid.*, p. 360: "Notwithstanding the constant reiteration of unity and solidarity, the New World has preserved as much international anarchy and achieved no more political integration than despised Europe."
[24] *Ibid.*, p. 6.

Pearl Harbor, and their lines have never been reformed. Conversely, that attack and the entry of the United States into the war as a full-fledged participant brought to power those interventionists who were sworn enemies to the "western hemisphere complex."

Their victory marked the completion of that revolution in public opinion and policy by which, in the short space of four years, globalism supplanted the traditional hemispheric faith. It was a revolution from above, but the war made it popular. As early as 1943 the new mood was so prevalent that Walter Lippmann, the most widely read of American foreign policy pundits, could say as a matter of course that the most important foreign relations of the United States had *always* been with Britain, Russia, and China.[25]

The revolution against the Western Hemisphere idea has been discussed at length because the revolutionists' victory over it was definitive. Subsequent developments have made it increasingly unlikely that the issue will be reopened. Quite aside from those developments whose global implications affect all countries, such as the atomic and hydrogen bombs, there have been several of special and great concern to the United States, such as the continual expansion of its economic interests outside the Western Hemisphere.

Take the case of the giant General Motors Corporation, which is a leader in both civilian and defense production. Since 1945 General Motors has doubled its net worth and built up an industrial empire on which the sun never sets. Of the

[25] Walter Lippmann, *U.S. Foreign Policy: Shield of the Republic* (New York, 1943), p. 161: "For more than a century, whenever our vital interests were at stake, American foreign relations have always been primarily our relations with Britain, with Russia, and with China." Significantly, Lippmann repeated the myth that the Monroe Doctrine rested upon a prior agreement between the United States and Britain (*ibid.*, pp. 16–18), although President Roosevelt had already (on December 29, 1940) exploded this myth, which no qualified historian accepted, in one of his most important public addresses (Bemis, *John Quincy Adams,* p. 401).

eighteen plants which it had built outside the United States by 1953, only five were in the Western Hemisphere; four were in England, two in Australia, and one each in Belgium, Denmark, Sweden, South Africa, India, Java, and New Zealand. Or take the case of petroleum, which the United States consumes in far greater volume than any other country in the world, and which has become indispensable to it for both peace and war. Since 1948 the United States has been, on balance, an importer of petroleum, and most of the world's known supply of it outside the United States is concentrated in Iran and other parts of the Middle East. Former isolationists have modified their stand accordingly. Thus, when in 1951 former President Hoover came out in favor of the Gibraltar of the Western Hemisphere, he provided it with flying buttresses in the British Isles and Japan.

First fruits of revolution: Globalism

Several major policy developments of the past decade have been nothing more than a working out of the implications of the revolutionists' victory over the Western Hemisphere complex in the early 1940's. Only the main outlines of the process can be indicated here. The following sketch of it is intended to be merely descriptive and not to pass judgment on the policy questions involved.

It falls into two parts divided by the end of the United Nations Conference at San Francisco in June 1945. The theme of the first period was the triumph of globalism; that of the second period was its prompt and resounding collapse and its replacement by new and different two-world concepts. In both periods the auxiliary engine of Pan Americanism was given new parts and a high polish, but the discarded Western Hemisphere idea continued to gather dust.

In the first period the issue of isolation versus intervention was replaced by a new issue, the character of the new world-wide organization which was to come out of the war. Here that surviving child of the Western Hemisphere idea, Pan Americanism, was involved. Though handicapped by the isolationist stigma pinned upon it by Spykman and others, it seemed likely at first that Pan Americanism would fare rather well both as to procedure and content in the planning of the new organization. The United States and Britain were sure to have an important influence in both respects, and at the outset their chief spokesmen in these matters were, respectively, Under Secretary Sumner Welles, an ardent Pan Americanist who had, however, never been an isolationist, and Prime Minister Winston Churchill, who early in 1943 proposed that the world organization be set up on a regional basis, with a "Council for Europe" and a "Council for Asia," and, it was implied, with the already existing Pan American system serving as a "Council for America." At this stage President Roosevelt, too, was sympathetic to the regional plan: he was on terms of personal friendship with both Churchill and Welles; and only a few years back he had led in singing hosannas to the Hemispheric idea.

Secretary Hull, however, objected to the regional plan, partly, as he tells us, because he feared that the projected Council for America would become "a haven for isolationists." In the spring of 1943 he took direct charge of the planning so far as the United States was concerned, supplanting Welles, and in August the latter resigned as Under Secretary of State. By that time Hull and his like-minded advisers had talked Roosevelt around to the more highly centralized type of organization which they preferred; and Churchill, too, was converted. The story is told in considerable detail in Hull's *Memoirs*,[26] but these leave many questions unanswered, including some relating to motivation, above all with regard to the Soviet Union. It seems likely that thoughts about the

[26] Hull, *op. cit.*, II, 1634–1648.

Soviet Union powerfully influenced the determination of Washington to play down regionalism in the United Nations. These thoughts combined suspicion of the misuse which Moscow might make of regional arrangements in Europe and Asia with the desire to allay Soviet suspicion regarding the misuse that the United States might make of them in the Western Hemisphere.

There were, of course, other reasons as well. For one thing, earlier discussions of a similar problem in the League of Nations days had convinced many persons of influence and authority that effective regionalism was incompatible with effective general international organization. In the particular case of American regionalism, this opinion was strengthened by wartime dissension which broke out within the Pan American family and fostered skepticism about its value as an international unit.

This dissension was aroused mainly, though not solely, by the conduct of neutralist, pro-Axis Argentina. By an unfortunate coincidence, the Argentine case came to a head in 1943–1944, just as the three Great Powers entered upon the crucial phase of their planning for a general international organization. Secretary of State Hull decided to crack down on the Buenos Aires regime for violating its Pan American commitments, but that required economic sanctions, which could not be effective without British co-operation. To the British, this meant shutting off precious supplies of beef which could be replaced only by pork from the United States, and the British took a dim view of the proposed exchange. The *Manchester Guardian* put it bluntly: "We like the Argentine brand of Fascism as little as does Mr. Cordell Hull, but we also prefer Argentine beef to American pork." [27] British support of the

[27] Arthur P. Whitaker, ed., *Inter-American Affairs, 1944* (New York, 1945), p. 19. For two contrasting accounts of a background episode involving divergent views of Western Hemisphere unity, see Hull, *op. cit.*, II, ch. lxxxviii, "Neighbors and War," and Sumner Welles, *Seven Decisions That Shaped*

sanctions was not forthcoming. The result was a deadlock which had not been ended when, because of ill health, Hull resigned as Secretary of State in November 1944. One striking feature of this affair was the failure of the Pan American system to work for lack of the co-operation of a non-American power.

The development of this "Argentine brand of Fascism" also illustrates a widespread trend in Latin America which undermined one of the fundamental assumptions of the Western Hemisphere idea. As stated in 1908 by A. C. Coolidge in his book *The United States as a World Power*, from which we have already quoted, the assumption in question was to the effect that "the New World differed from the Old . . . in being the home of free governments in contrast to the lands ruled by the principle of authority." In the half-century before 1930 this belief had been strengthened by the substantial progress which was made toward the development of liberal, stable governments in Latin America. After 1930, however, so large a part of the area relapsed into revolution and dictatorship that faith gave way to skepticism. One of the most disillusioning cases was that of Argentina. Third in population but first in wealth and literacy, Argentina had by the 1920's also become first among the Latin American states in the development of stable democratic government. Yet that country fell victim to one military coup in 1930 and to another in 1943, and out of the latter grew the stabilized tyranny of the Perón regime. After 1945 there was about as much authoritarianism in the New World as in the Old (meaning Europe), and about as much freedom in the Old World as in the New. The traditional dichotomy had disappeared, taking with it the heart of the Western Hemisphere idea.

These circumstances and considerations should make more

History (New York, 1951), ch. iv, "The Decision That Saved New World Unity."

comprehensible the abrupt reversal of the attitude of the United States toward American regionalism. The new attitude was exemplified in connection with the Dumbarton Oaks Proposals for a United Nations charter, which were drawn up in 1944 by the four great powers (Britain, the Soviet Union, the United States, and China). In contrast with Britain, whose Prime Minister Churchill and Foreign Secretary Eden discussed the preliminaries of the Dumbarton Oaks meeting with representatives of the Commonwealth governments, Washington steadily refused repeated requests from Latin America for a Pan American consultation on this subject. In contrast with the frequent Pan American conferences and meetings of foreign ministers in the immediately preceding period (in 1936, 1938, 1939, 1940, and January 1942), there was not a single such consultation in the three crucial years from February 1942 to February 1945, when the Chapultepec Conference was held as a curtain raiser to the impending United Nations Conference at San Francisco.

Pan American revival in Latin America

For a time, as leadership in and enthusiasm for American regionalism declined in the United States, it rose in Latin America,[28] which produced a more substantial defense of American regionalism against such writers as Spykman and Lippmann than any that came out of the United States.[29] An illustration of the new attitude of the Latin Americans has been their persistent effort in the postwar years to employ the American regional system as an agency in hastening the final ejection of Europe from America, that is, to liquidate the last

[28] Arthur P. Whitaker, "The Role of Latin America in Relation to Current Trends in International Organization," *American Political Science Review,* XXXIX (1945), 503–511. Reproduced, with omission of the first section and footnotes, in Asher N. Christensen, ed., *The Evolution of Latin American Government: A Book of Readings* (New York, 1951), pp. 711–721.

[29] This was Jesús M. Yepes, *La philosophie du Panaméricanisme.*

171

remaining European colonies in America—those of Britain, France, and the Netherlands. The United States has opposed the effort on the ground that this is a problem for the United Nations, but the Latin Americans have insisted time and again since 1945 in attacking it through the Inter-American system.

There were several reasons for the Latin Americans' new attitude. For one thing, during the war they realized that in the postwar years they would urgently need financial and other assistance and that only the United States would be able to provide this on a large scale; and recent experience had taught them that the Pan American system was a useful instrument for obtaining benefits of this kind. The new mood was well expressed in a book by Mexican Foreign Minister Ezequiel Padilla, published in an English translation under the title *Free Men of America* (1943), in which he proposed the creation of a Pan American economic union designed mainly to free the men of Latin America, with the aid of the United States, from the competition of servile labor in Asia and Africa.

Another reason for their new attitude was the Latin Americans' dislike and suspicion of the Soviet Union. Mistrusting the use Moscow might make of the great-power veto to hamstring security measures for any purpose but its own, they fought to salvage an effective Pan American system in the United Nations Conference at San Francisco. This they largely accomplished by writing into the United Nations Charter provisions for security action by regional and other limited groups.

Of course, this change could not have been made had it not been strongly urged by other countries as well, and for other reasons, and acquiesced in by the great powers. The acquiescence of the United States was due in large measure to the influence of one of its chief delegates, Senator Arthur

Vandenberg, a former isolationist who retained his prewar
affection for the Pan American system.[30] Yet even Senator
Vandenberg no longer adhered to the Western Hemisphere
idea in its pristine purity. To him as to the rest of the government and the public at large, Pan Americanism was now
merely one of several instruments to be used in keeping the
world in order; it was to be subordinated to the United Nations so long as the latter served its purpose and to be used
as second line of defense only if the United Nations failed to
function properly.

Iron curtain and Northern Hemisphere

This view was only reinforced by the schism soon brought
about in the global structure by Soviet intransigence. The
incidents that marked the split began almost at once with the
fiasco of the great-power meeting of Foreign Ministers at
London in October 1945 and continued to grow with the
successive crises over Iran, Greece, Czechoslovakia, Berlin,
and Korea.

A new two-world concept now took shape, supplanting the
one-world dream which in its turn had supplanted the Hemisphere idea in the early 1940's. Now the two worlds were
not the hemispheres but the communist slave world and the
noncommunist free world; the dividing line between them
ran not up and down the Atlantic but along the Iron Curtain;
and the anti-European bias of the Western Hemisphere idea
gave way to the conception of Western Europe as the natural
and indispensable ally of America in the community of free-
world nations.

The reorientation has been abundantly illustrated in the
cold-war years, beginning in March 1947 with the Truman
Doctrine, which, with its promise of aid to Greece and Turkey,
"launched the United States upon a positive program of re-

[30] Sumner Welles, *Where Are We Heading?* p. 19.

sisting the expansionist tactics of international commu-
nism." [31] Perhaps through a kind of ancestor worship, the
Truman Doctrine was described as globalizing the Monroe
Doctrine; but the description only showed how completely the
Western Hemisphere idea had been forgotten, for the very
essence of the Monroe Doctrine was its exclusively Western
Hemisphere character. Again, when the Marshall Plan for
Europe was adopted in 1947, the good neighbors to the south
promptly set up a cry for a Marshall Plan for Latin America,
invoking the old "special relationship" of the Western Hemisphere idea; but the answer from Washington was no, and it
was given with an air of pained surprise as if the special
relationship, too, had been forgotten.

Short of a Soviet conquest of all the Old World, there seems
no reason to expect a revival of the Hemisphere idea such
as occurred during the years of disillusionment that followed
the failure of Woodrow Wilson's League of Nations effort.
The temper of the times has changed too greatly since then
—how greatly is suggested by the fact that although similar
disappointment with the United Nations led to a strengthening of Western Hemisphere defense through the Rio de
Janeiro Treaty of 1947, this was promptly followed and completely overshadowed by the creation of the North Atlantic
Treaty Organization.[32] Including among its members both
Canada and the United States, NATO links nearly half the
area and more than half the population of America to Western Europe in an alliance that is incompatible with the historic Western Hemisphere idea, an essential element of which
was the separation of America from Europe.

[31] Francis O. Wilcox and Thorsten V. Kalijarvi, *Recent American Foreign
Policy: Basic Documents 1941–1951* (New York, 1952), p. 814, introductory
note to the text of the Truman Doctrine, which follows, pp. 814–819.

[32] *Ibid.*, pp. 208–214 (Rio Treaty), 868–873 (North Atlantic Treaty).
Maps showing the areas covered by these two treaties are given on pp. 214
and 870.

Another sign of the times was the displacement of the term "Western Hemisphere" by "Northern Hemisphere." To be sure, displacement did not mean abandonment, at least so far as policy pronouncements were concerned. Whether deliberately for diplomatic reasons, or unconsciously from force of habit, government spokesmen went on repeating the Western Hemisphere shibboleth even when, by their own showing, it was only a shibboleth.

An example is provided by former Secretary of State Dean Acheson's address of December 30, 1951, reviewing foreign policy developments of the past year.[33] He began with a brief nod to "the Western Hemisphere," which he described as "the foundation of our position in the world." But later he modified this by the more realistic description of "our position" as one "lying in both the Western and Northern Hemispheres"; and in fact almost all of his address dealt with areas of the Northern and Eastern Hemispheres—with Western Europe, the Near and Middle East, and the Far East. The politico-geographical idea underlying this address was fundamentally different from the idea whose history we have sketched in these pages, and there can be no doubt that, on this point, Secretary Acheson voiced the views now held by the great majority of his fellow countrymen.

Pan American agencies and measures have indeed survived, and have even continued their glacier-like growth. Outstanding evidences include, besides the Western Hemisphere Defense Treaty of 1947, the Charter of the Organization of American States, adopted the following year, and the emergency meeting of American foreign ministers held early in 1951 to meet the crisis caused by Red China's entry into the Korean war. Their continued growth has been possible, however, only because these agencies and measures have been dissociated from the politico-geographical idea which, in an

[33] Full text in *New York Times*, December 31, 1951.

earlier and far different age, first begot American regionalism and because they have been integrated into a conceptual framework of global proportions in which the Western Hemisphere has lost its historic identity.

The idea has always found its best expression in the realm of politics and diplomacy. Whatever one may think of the results attained in that realm, they provide most of the evidence that can be adduced in support of the proposition that the peoples of America are bound together in a special relationship which sets them apart from the rest of the world. In other fields, such as the cultural, comparable evidence would be hard to find. For example, in the basic matter of language the Americas have remained divided into three major groups, English, Spanish, and Portuguese, which in this respect have closer ties with Europe than with one another. The very currents of thought which have done most to create a common American climate of opinion, such as the eighteenth-century Enlightenment and nineteenth-century positivism, were importations from Europe and in the long run strengthened trans-Atlantic as well as hemispheric ties. More broadly, despite several centuries of the common experience of development in a New World environment, the history of the Americas has so far successfully resisted the efforts of American historians to integrate it in accordance with the Western Hemisphere idea. Save in the political realm, the record of that experience is largely one which is held together either by the common ties of the Americas with Europe or else by the covers of a book.

Though realized on a substantial scale only in the realm of politics and diplomacy, the Western Hemisphere idea has served a useful purpose. The isolationist tinge which it exhibited in the 1930's belied its earlier record. Throughout most of its history it has served the opposite purpose of promoting a limited kind of internationalism in countries where isolationism was strong, such as the United States and Argentina. For these and all the other American countries it has long provided a laboratory and proving ground for policies, institutions, and experiences that were later applied with advantage in the broader field of world affairs.[34]

[34] Arthur P. Whitaker, "Our Pan American Policy and the Post-War World," *Harvard Educational Review,* XIII (1943), 285–300.

List of Works Cited

THE following list contains only the books and articles cited in the footnotes of the present study. As stated in the Preface, the citations are intended only to acknowledge my indebtedness for direct quotations and important information and ideas and to serve as signposts to the many other relevant sources and secondary works. The items are arranged in alphabetical order according to the name of the author or editor, without distinguishing between sources and secondary works or books and articles. Preference has been given to works in English, but it is believed that there is a fair sampling of the literature on the Latin American side. The comparatively large number of items under my own name may be excused on the ground that they explain and document more fully some of the views sketched in these essays.

Further exploration among the multitudinous works relating to the subjects discussed in this study should begin with such well known bibliographical aids as Bemis and Griffin, *Guide to the Diplomatic History of the United States, 1775–1921;* the annuals *Handbook of Latin American Studies* and *Writings on American*

History; and the quarterly *Foreign Affairs* and other publications of the Council on Foreign Relations (New York).

Adler, Selig. "Bryan and Wilsonian Caribbean Penetration," *Hispanic American Historical Review,* XX (1940), 198–226.

Armstrong, Hamilton Fish, Jr., ed. *The Foreign Affairs Reader.* New York, 1947.

Bailey, Thomas A. *The United States and the Neutrals.* Baltimore, 1948.

——. *Woodrow Wilson and the Lost Peace.* New York, 1945.

Barager, Joseph R. "Sarmiento and the United States." MS, doctoral dissertation, 1951, University of Pennsylvania Library.

Barcia Trelles, Camilo. "Doctrina de Monroe y cooperación internacional," Académie de Droit International, *Recueil des cours, 1930,* II (Paris, 1931), 391–605.

Barreda Laos, Felipe. *Hispano América en guerra?* Buenos Aires, 1941.

Bartlett, Ruhl J., ed. *The Record of American Diplomacy.* New York, 1947.

Basadre, Jorge. *Perú: Problema y posibilidad.* Lima, 1931.

Beard, Charles A. *A Foreign Policy for the United States.* New York, 1940.

Becker, Carl. *The Heavenly City of the Eighteenth-Century Philosophers.* New Haven, 1932.

Belaúnde, Víctor Andrés. *Bolívar and the Political Thought of the Spanish American Revolution.* Baltimore, 1930.

Bemis, Samuel F. *A Diplomatic History of the United States.* Rev. ed. New York, 1942.

——. *John Quincy Adams and the Foundations of American Foreign Policy.* New York, 1949.

——. *The Latin American Policy of the United States: An Historical Interpretation.* New York, 1943.

Bernstein, Harry. *Origins of Inter-American Interest, 1700–1812.* Philadelphia, 1945.

Bidwell, Percy W. *Economic Defense of Latin America.* Boston, 1941.

Bierck, Harold A., Jr. *Vida pública de don Pedro Gual*. Caracas, 1947.

Bolton, Herbert E. *Wider Horizons of American History*. New York, 1939.

Bonsal, Stephen. *Unfinished Business*. New York, 1944.

Borchard, E. M. "Calvo and Drago Doctrines," *Encyclopaedia of the Social Sciences*, vol. III. New York, 1930.

Bornholdt, Laura. "The Abbé de Pradt and the Monroe Doctrine," *Hispanic American Historical Review*, XXIV (1944), 201–221.

Bowers, Claude G. *Beveridge and the Progressive Era*. Boston, 1932.

Brooks, C. E. P. "What Is Happening to the Weather?" *Harper's Magazine*, January 1953, pp. 32–39.

Bunkley, Allison W. *The Life of Sarmiento*. Princeton, 1952.

——, ed. *A Sarmiento Anthology*. Princeton, 1948.

Burr, Robert N., and Roland D. Hussey, eds. *Documents on Inter-American Cooperation, 1810–1881*. [Philadelphia, 1955.]

Calmon, Pedro. *Historia de la civilización brasileña*. Buenos Aires, 1938.

Caruso, John Anthony. "The Pan American Railway," *Hispanic American Historical Review*, XXXI (1951), 608–639.

Cassirer, Ernst. *The Philosophy of the Enlightenment*. Princeton, 1951.

Cavelier, Germán. *La política internacional de Colombia . . . (1820–1830)*. Bogotá, 1949.

Chase, Stuart. *The New Western Front*. New York, 1939.

Chinard, Gilbert. "Eighteenth Century Theories on America as a Human Habitat," American Philosophical Society, *Proceedings*, XCI, no. 1 (1947), 27–57.

Christensen, Asher N., ed. *The Evolution of Latin American Government: A Book of Readings*. New York, 1951.

Concolorcorvo. *El lazarillo de ciegos caminantes*. Paris, 1938. (Biblioteca de Cultura Peruana, Primera Série, no. 6.)

Coolidge, Archibald Cary. "The Grouping of Nations," *Foreign Affairs*, V (1927), 175–188.

——. *The United States as a World Power*. New York, 1908.

Crawford, W. Rex. *A Century of Latin American Thought.* Cambridge, Mass., 1944.

Cuevas Cancino, Francisco. *Bolívar: El ideal panamericano del Liberatador.* Mexico City, 1951.

Curti, Merle. *The Growth of American Thought.* New York, 1943.

DeConde, Alexander. *Herbert Hoover's Latin American Policy.* Stanford, 1951.

Department of State. *The Lansing Papers, 1914–1920.* 2 vols. Washington, D.C., 1940.

——. *Papers Relating to the Foreign Relations of the United States, 1903.* Washington, D.C., 1904.

——. *Ibid., 1928.* Washington, D.C., 1942.

Drago, Mariano J. *Luis Drago, discursos y escritos.* 3 vols. Buenos Aires, 1938.

Duggan, Laurence. *The Americas: The Search for Hemisphere Security.* New York, 1949.

Earle, Edward M. "A Half-Century of American Foreign Policy, 1898–1948," *Political Science Quarterly,* LXIV (1949), 168–188.

Ensayos sobre la historia del Nuevo Mundo. Mexico, 1951. (Publication no. 31 of the Commission on History, Pan American Institute of Geography and History.)

Feis, Herbert. "The Export of American Capital," *Foreign Affairs,* III (1925), 668–686.

Ferris, Nathan L. "The Relations of the United States with South America during the Civil War," *Hispanic American Historical Review,* XXI (1941), 51–78.

Frank, Jerome. *Save America First.* New York, 1938.

Frazer, Robert N. "Latin American Projects to Aid Mexico During the French Intervention," *Hispanic American Historical Review,* XXVIII (1948), 377–388.

——. "The Role of the Lima Congress, 1864–1865, in the Development of Pan-Americanism," *Hispanic American Historical Review,* XXIX (1949), 319–348.

Friede, Juan. "El arraigo histórico del espíritu de la independencia en el Nuevo Reino de Granada," *Revista de Historia de América,* no. 33 (1952), 95–104.

Gabriel, Ralph H. *The Course of American Democratic Thought.* New York, 1940.

Gantenbein, James W. *The Evolution of Our Latin American Policy: A Documentary Record.* New York, 1950.

García Samudio, Nicolás. *Independencia de Hispanoamérica.* Mexico City, 1945.

Gerbi, Antonello. *Viejas polémicas sobre el nuevo mundo.* 3d ed. Lima, 1946.

Gershoy, Leo. *From Despotism to Revolution, 1763–1789.* New York, 1944.

Gil, Enrique. *Evolución del Panamericanismo.* Buenos Aires, 1933.

Giménez Fernández, Manuel. *Las doctrinas populistas en la independencia de Hispano-América.* Seville, 1947.

Graham, Malbone W. *American Diplomacy in the International Community.* Baltimore, 1948.

Guerrant, Edward O. *Roosevelt's Good Neighbor Policy.* Albuquerque, 1950.

Hayes, Carleton J. H. *A Generation of Materialism, 1871–1900.* New York, 1941.

Hazard, Paul. *La pensée européene au XVIIIème siècle.* Paris, 1946.

Henríquez-Ureña, Pedro. *Literary Currents in Hispanic America.* Cambridge, Mass., 1945.

Hernández de Alba, Guillermo. "Origen de la doctrina panamericana de la confederación," *Revista de Historia de América,* no. 22 (1946), 367–398.

Historical Appendix. See *International American Conference.*

Hofstadter, Richard. *Social Darwinism in American Thought, 1860–1915.* Philadelphia, 1945.

Hughes, Charles Evans. *Our Relations to the Nations of the Western Hemisphere.* Princeton, 1928.

Hull, Cordell. *Memoirs of Cordell Hull.* 2 vols. New York, 1948.

Humphrey, John P. *The Inter-American System: A Canadian View.* Toronto, 1942.

International American Conference, *Reports of Committees,* vol.

IV, *Historical Appendix: The Congress of 1826 at Panama and Subsequent Movements Towards a Conference of American Nations.* Washington, D.C., 1890.

Jessup, Philip C. *Elihu Root.* 2 vols. New York, 1938.

Johnson, Walter. *The Battle Against Isolation.* Chicago, 1944.

Kelchner, Warren H. *Latin American Relations with the League of Nations.* Boston, 1929.

Klein, Julius. "Economic Rivalries in Latin America," *Foreign Affairs,* III (1924), 236–243.

Kraus, Michael. *The Atlantic Civilization: Eighteenth-Century Origins.* Ithaca, 1949.

Langer, William L. *The Diplomacy of Imperialism, 1890–1902.* New York, 1935.

——. "Political Problems of a Coalition," *Foreign Affairs,* XXVI (1947), 73–89.

——, and S. Everett Gleason. *The Challenge to Isolation, 1937–1940.* New York, 1952.

Lecuna, Vicente. *Cartas del Libertador.* 11 vols. Caracas, 1929–1930, 1948.

Leuchtenburg, William E. "Progressivism and Imperialism: the Progressive Movement and American Foreign Policy, 1898–1916," *Mississippi Valley Historical Review,* XXXIX (1952), 483–504.

Lewis, Cleona. *America's Stake in International Investments.* Washington, D.C., 1938.

Link, Arthur S. *Woodrow Wilson and the Progressive Era, 1910–1917.* New York, 1954.

Lippmann, Walter. *U.S. Foreign Policy: Shield of the Republic.* New York, 1943.

Lobo, Helio. *O Pan-americanismo e o Brasil.* São Paulo, 1939.

Lockey, Joseph B. *Pan Americanism: Its Beginnings.* New York, 1920.

Lovett, Robert Morss. "American Foreign Policy: A Progressive View," *Foreign Affairs,* III (1924), 49–60.

Mackinder, Halford J. *Democratic Ideals and Reality.* New York, 1942.

McNicoll, Robert E. "Intellectual Origins of Aprismo," *Hispanic American Historical Review*, XXIII (1943), 424–440.

Masur, Gerhard. *Simón Bolívar*. Albuquerque, 1948.

Miner, Dwight C. *The Fight for the Panama Route*. New York, 1940.

Moore, John Bassett. *The Principles of American Diplomacy*. New York, 1918.

Morison, S. E., and Henry S. Commager, *The Growth of the American Republic*. New York, 1937.

Morse, Richard M. "Toward a Theory of Spanish American Government," *Journal of the History of Ideas*, XV (1954), 71–93.

Motten, Clement G. *Mexican Silver and the Enlightenment*. Philadelphia, 1950.

Notter, Harley. *The Origins of the Foreign Policy of Woodrow Wilson*. Baltimore, 1937.

Nuermberger, Gustave A. "The Continental Treaties of 1856," *Hispanic American Historical Review*, XX (1940), 32–55.

Pan American Scientific Congress (Second). *Proceedings*, vol. VII. Washington, D.C., 1917.

Perkins, Dexter. *The American Approach to Foreign Policy*. Upsala and Stockholm, 1949.

——. *The Monroe Doctrine, 1823–1826*. Cambridge, Mass., 1932.

——. *The Monroe Doctrine, 1867–1907*. Baltimore, 1937.

Pratt, Julius W. *The Expansionists of 1898*. Baltimore, 1936.

Pusey, Merlo J. *Charles Evans Hughes*. 2 vols. New York, 1951.

Rauch, Basil. *Roosevelt from Munich to Pearl Harbor*. New York, 1950.

Register of Debates in Congress, 1824–1837. 14 vols. Washington, 1825–1837.

Richardson, James D., ed. *Messages and Papers of the Presidents*. Washington, 1896–1899. Vol. II.

Rippy, J. Fred. *Latin America and the Industrial Age*. 2d ed. New York, 1947.

——. *Latin America in World Politics*. 3d ed. New York, 1938.

——. *Rivalry of the United States and Great Britain over Latin America, 1808–1830*. Baltimore, 1929.

——. "Argentina," in A. C. Wilgus, ed., *Argentina, Brazil and Chile since Independence*. Washington, D.C., 1935.

——, and Angie Debo, "The Historical Background of the American Policy of Isolation," *Smith College Studies in History*, IX (1924), 71–165.

Robertson, William Spence. *Hispanic American Relations with the United States*. New York, 1923.

Rojas, Ricardo. *El profeta de la pampa: Vida de Sarmiento*. Buenos Aires, 1945.

Roosevelt, Franklin D. "Our Foreign Policy," *Foreign Affairs*, VI (1928), 573–586.

Roosevelt, Theodore. *The Letters of Theodore Roosevelt*. Ed. by Elting E. Morison. Cambridge, Mass., 1951–. Vol. III.

Root, Elihu. *Latin America and the United States: Addresses*. Cambridge, Mass., 1917.

Sánchez, Luis-Alberto. "A New Interpretation of the History of America," *Hispanic American Historical Review*, XXIII (1943), 441–456.

Scott, F. R. *Canada and the United States*. Boston, 1941.

Shepardson, Whitney H., and William O. Scroggs, *The United States in World Affairs, 1939*. New York, 1940.

Silva, Carlos Alberto. *La política internacional de la Argentina*. Buenos Aires, 1946.

Sprout, Harold and Margaret. *Toward a New Order of Sea Power, 1918–1922*. New York, 1940.

Spykman, Nicholas John. *America's Strategy in World Politics*. New York, 1942.

Staley, Eugene. "The Myth of the Continents," *Foreign Affairs*, XIX (1941), 481–494.

Stimson, Henry L., and McGeorge Bundy. *On Active Service in Peace and War*. New York, 1948.

Tyler, Alice Felt. *The Foreign Policy of James G. Blaine*. Minneapolis, 1927.

Ulloa, Alberto. *Congresos americanos de Lima*. 2 vols. Lima, 1938.

Weinberg, Albert K. "The Historical Meaning of the Doctrine of Isolation," *American Political Science Review*, XXIV (1940), 542 ff.

Weinberg, Albert K. *Manifest Destiny: A Study of Nationalist Expansion in American History*. Baltimore, 1935.

Welles, Sumner. *Naboth's Vineyard: The Dominican Republic, 1844–1924*. 2 vols. New York, 1928.

———. *Seven Decisions That Shaped History*. New York, 1951.

———. *The Time for Decision*. New York, 1944.

———. *Where Are We Heading?* New York, 1946.

———. *The World of the Four Freedoms*. New York, 1943.

Whitaker, Arthur P. "The Elhuyar Mining Missions and the Enlightenment," *Hispanic American Historical Review*, XXXI (1951), 557–585.

———. "From Dollar Diplomacy to the Good Neighbor Policy," *Inter-American Economic Affairs*, IV (1951), 12–19.

———. "Our Pan American Policy and the Post-War World," *Harvard Educational Review*, XIII (1943), 285–300.

———. "The Role of Latin America in Relation to Current Trends in International Organization," *American Political Science Review*, XXXIX (1945), 503–511.

———. "Three Autobiographies," *Appel Memorial Lectures*. Lancaster, Pa., 1950.

———. *The United States and the Independence of Latin America*. Baltimore, 1941.

———, ed. *Inter-American Affairs: An Annual Survey, 1941–1945*. 5 vols. New York, 1942–1946.

———, ed. *Latin America and the Enlightenment*. New York, 1942.

Wilcox, Francis O., and Thorsten V. Kalijarvi, eds. *Recent American Foreign Policy: Basic Documents, 1941–1951*. New York, 1951.

Wilgus, A. C., ed. *Argentina, Brazil and Chile since Independence*. Washington, D.C., 1935.

———. "Blaine and Pan Americanism," *Hispanic American Historical Review*, V (1922), 662–708.

Winkler, Max. *Investments of United States Capital in Latin America*. Boston, 1928.

Woodward, E. L., and Rohan Butler, eds. *Documents on British Foreign Policy, 1919–1939*. 2d ser., vol. I. London, 1946.

Wythe, George. *Industry in Latin America*. New York, 1945.

Yepes, Jesús M. *La philosophie du panaméricanisme*. Neuchâtel, 1945.

Zavala, Silvio. *La filosofía política en la conquista de América*. Mexico City, 1947.

———. *La Utopia de Tomás More en la Nueva España y otros estudios*. Mexico City, 1937.

Zea, Leopoldo. *América como conciencia*. Mexico City, 1953.

———. *Dos etapas del pensamiento en Hispanoamérica: del romanticismo al positivismo*. Mexico City, 1949.

Index